Wales
AND
Britain

in the Medieval World

c1000 – c1500

Hefin Mathias

Hodder & Stoughton
A MEMBER OF THE HODDER HEADLINE GROUP

Acknowledgements

The cover shows a portrait of Sion Cent, from a private collection.

Hulton Deutsch Collection 4a; Michael Holford Photographs 10a, 12a; Wales Tourist Board 17d, 21b; Hunting Aerofilms Limited 18c; Photographie Bulloz 25f; The President and Fellows of Corpus Christi College, Oxford 26a (CCC MS 157 f.382-383); By permission of The British Library 27d (Henry II quarrelling with Thomas Becket), 29e (a thirteenth-century crusading knight, MS 2A XXII f.220), 49c (picture of the siege of Mortagne from the Chronicle d'Angleterre, MS Royal 14 EIV f.23), 50b (image of the Great Death, MS Arundel 83 f.127), 53e (King Richard II meeting Wat Tyler at Smithfield, MS Royal 18 EI f.175), 60b (illustration of a ploughman from the Luttrell Psalter, Add42130 f.170), 61c (portrait of William Herbert, MS Royal 18 DII f.6); La Bibliothèque Nationale 28a (MS 9087 f.85v), 30c (Fr 2620 f.22v); Mirror Syndication International © Macmillan/Aldus 30d; Mary Evans Picture Library 32a; The Master and Fellows of Corpus Christi College, Cambridge 32b (CCC MS 16 f.44v), 55g (CCC MS 61); The Royal Collection , Her Majesty The Queen 37c (MS Harl 1319 f.57); Cardiff City Council 39i; Cadw: Welsh Historic Monuments. Crown Copyright. 42a, 42b, 43c, 58a, 58d; drawing by Arthur Morus 45f; Glamorgan Gwent Archaeological Trust Limited 46a; Hefin Mathias 47d, 47e; The Ancient Art and Architecture Collection 48a; The Archbishop of Canterbury and the Trustees of Lambeth Palace Library 54c; The National Library of Wales 57d.

Every effort has been made to trace and acknowledge ownership of copyright. The publishers will be glad to make suitable arrangements with any copyright holders whom it has not been possible to contact.

Orders: please contact Bookpoint Ltd, 39 Milton Park, Abingdon, Oxon OX14 4TD. Telephone: (44) 01235 400414, Fax: (44) 01235 400454. Lines are open from 9.00 – 6.00, Monday to Saturday, with a 24 hour message answering service. Email address: orders@bookpoint.co.uk

British Library Cataloguing in Publication Data

A catalogue for this title is available from the British Library

ISBN 0340 63149 X

First published 1996
Impression number   11 10 9 8 7 6 5 4 3 2
Year   2004 2003 2002 2001 2000 1999 1998

This book is published with the financial support of the Curriculum and Assessment Authority for Wales

Typeset by The University of Wales, Aberystwyth, Wales
Printed in Hong Kong for Hodder & Stoughton Educational, a division of Hodder Headline Plc, 338 Euston Road, London NW1 3BH by Colorcraft Ltd.

Contents

I *W*hat were Wales and England like in 1000?

A A portrait of Gerald

This is a book about Wales in the Middle Ages. This period in history was very different from our own. How do we know about the way people lived and the events that took place at that time? A great deal of our knowledge is based on the writings of a man named Gerald of Wales.

You can see a picture of Gerald (source A) taken from an old **manuscript**. In 1188 he journeyed through Wales. After completing the journey, he wrote two books, *Journey Through Wales* and a *Description of Wales*. These books are known as primary sources because they were written at the time of the event.

Gerald was alive during during the twelfth century, that is 1200 years after the birth of Christ. But what were Wales and the rest of the British Isles like 200 years earlier in the year 1000?

> *The Welsh people are light and agile. They are fierce rather than strong, and totally dedicated to the practice of arms. Not only their leaders but everyone in the nation are trained in war.*

 B Gerald's description of the Welsh people

1 Explain in your own words the meaning of the words 'primary source'.

2 (a) According to source B, what sort of people were the Welsh?
  (b) In what way does the map of the British Isles and the information given, support Gerald of Wales's description?

3 Read the descriptions, then draw the box opposite and place a tick below the countries which fit into each category.

	England	Wales	Ireland	Scotland
A Christian country				
A united country				
A disunited country				
A Celtic country				
A country invaded by the Vikings				

C A bird's eye view of the British Isles in the year 1000

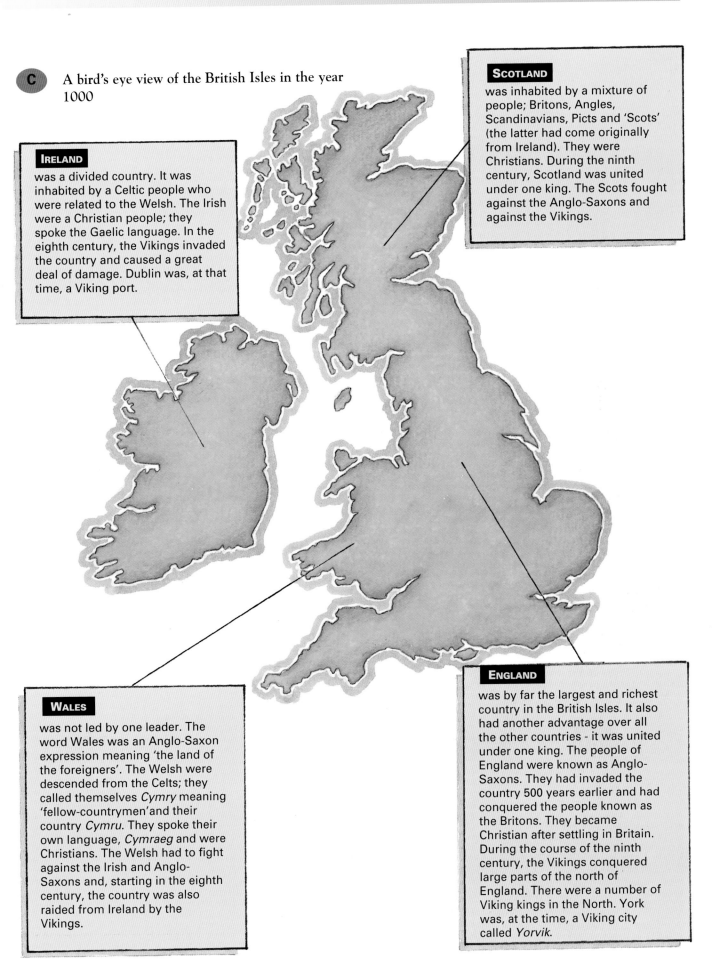

IRELAND

was a divided country. It was inhabited by a Celtic people who were related to the Welsh. The Irish were a Christian people; they spoke the Gaelic language. In the eighth century, the Vikings invaded the country and caused a great deal of damage. Dublin was, at that time, a Viking port.

SCOTLAND

was inhabited by a mixture of people; Britons, Angles, Scandinavians, Picts and 'Scots' (the latter had come originally from Ireland). They were Christians. During the ninth century, Scotland was united under one king. The Scots fought against the Anglo-Saxons and against the Vikings.

WALES

was not led by one leader. The word Wales was an Anglo-Saxon expression meaning 'the land of the foreigners'. The Welsh were descended from the Celts; they called themselves *Cymry* meaning 'fellow-countrymen'and their country *Cymru*. They spoke their own language, *Cymraeg* and were Christians. The Welsh had to fight against the Irish and Anglo-Saxons and, starting in the eighth century, the country was also raided from Ireland by the Vikings.

ENGLAND

was by far the largest and richest country in the British Isles. It also had another advantage over all the other countries - it was united under one king. The people of England were known as Anglo-Saxons. They had invaded the country 500 years earlier and had conquered the people known as the Britons. They became Christian after settling in Britain. During the course of the ninth century, the Vikings conquered large parts of the north of England. There were a number of Viking kings in the North. York was, at the time, a Viking city called *Yorvik*.

(above) **BRENIN** (THE KING)
He had to protect his kingdom against invaders and was expected to lead his men into battle. In return for this, the king and his court could be fed and housed in any part of his kingdom, free of charge. He could also collect gifts in the form of land or animals. In Wales, kingdoms were often divided up between sons of descendants of the late king.

(above) **DISTAIN** (STEWARD), **OFFEIRIAD** (PRIEST), **PENCERDD** (CHIEF POET), **YNAD** (JUDGE)
The king had a number of officials to help him rule the country and they lived with him in his court. Only freemen could be appointed as the king's officials.

A closer look at Wales

Wales was divided into a number of **kingdoms**. The main ones were Gwynedd, Powys, Deheubarth, Morgannwg and Gwent. Within each kingdom, the king was a very important person. Everybody looked up to him. (See source A).

During the tenth century, Hywel ap Cadell, known widely as Hywel Dda, King of Deheubarth, had succeeded in bringing almost the whole of Wales under his rule. According to later tradition, at Whitland, in Deheubarth, Hywel held an important meeting where the laws of Wales were written down. These are known as the **Laws of Hywel Dda**. These laws stated that there were three types of crime: murder, arson and robbery. Criminals were punished by being forced to pay compensation to the victims. The compensation was known as *galanas*. The criminal's family was made responsible for paying the *galanas* in proportion to their relationship with the victim of the criminal.

However, Wales did not remain united for long. Disagreements arose and fighting followed. During the years following his death in 949, over 25 kings were killed in battle, the eyes of four more were pulled out and a further four were thrown into prison.

(above) **GWŶR RHYDD** (FREEMEN)
These were people of pure Welsh blood. They had the right to hunt, ride and to fight in battle.

(above) **TAEOGION** (BONDMEN)
The bondmen lived a very hard life. They could not leave their own district without permission. They spent their lives working in the fields and tending the farm animals. They also had to produce food for the king and the freemen.

Only a very powerful ruler could hope to unite Wales. One such leader was Gruffudd ap Llywelyn. He took control of Gwynedd, Powys and Deheubarth. He also fought against the English and, in 1056, forced the King of England, Edward the Confessor, to meet him on equal terms. Any powerful leader at this time was sure to make enemies. In the end, Gruffudd was betrayed and was killed by his own men in 1063.

Gruffydd ap Llywelyn, the head and shield and defender of the Welsh, fell through the treachery of his own men.

B Gerald of Wales: *Description of Wales*

Gruffydd, King of the Welsh, was killed by his subjects on 5th August, 1063, and his head and his ship's beak with its ornaments were sent to Earl Harold, who sent them on to King Edward.

C An extract from the *Anglo-Saxon Chronicle*

D A map of Wales showing the different kingdoms in 1000

1 Why do you think that King Hywel was called Hywel the Good?

2 (a) Explain the meaning of the words 'freeman' and 'bondman'.
  (b) How were they different from each other?

3 (a) Explain in your own words why the law relating to the land made it difficult to unite Wales?
  (b) Why would a Welsh king want to conquer other kingdoms?

4 (a) In what way does the *Anglo-Saxon Chronicle* support what Gerald says about the death of Gruffudd ap Llywelyn?
  (b) What additional information is given by the *Anglo-Saxon Chronicle*?

5 You are a freeman living in Wales during the reign of Hywel Dda. In your own words, answer these two questions:
  (a) What makes Wales different from other countries?
  (b) Why is Wales such a difficult country to unite?

A closer look at England

By the year 1000, England was a united kingdom, ruled by Ethelred II, nicknamed Ethelred the Unready, of the Royal House of Wessex.

At one time, England, like Wales, had been a divided country with three main kingdoms competing against each other - Wessex, Mercia and Northumbria. During the ninth century, Alfred, King of Wessex, united the Anglo-Saxons and came to an agreement with the Vikings.

Alfred defeated the invading Vikings and allowed them to live in the north of England, which came to be known as the *Danelaw*. Gradually, Alfred's successors won back the *Danelaw* from the Vikings. Towards the end of the tenth century the whole of England was united under one ruler, King Edgar. However, the Vikings returned to England in even greater numbers. Ethelred II the King of England, had to pay them to go away. This did not stop them.

Eventually, the Viking king Cnut took over the whole country and ruled England from 1016 until 1035. During this time, England lived in peace. Alfred the Great had set up local strongholds called **burhs**. During Cnut's reign, these burhs were developing into towns. London became the capital of this kingdom and trade began to grow.

(above) The king was expected to defend his kingdom and to lead his men into battle. To help him rule his kingdom, he had local officials called sheriffs. When a king died, his kingdom was passed on to his eldest son. The king had to be a man of strong character to keep hold of his kingdom. His wealth was based on food collected from noblemen, fines collected from people breaking the king's law and plunder gained as a result of military campaigns.

(above) The ordinary people belonged to two classes, the free and the unfree. Free persons were called **churls**. They lived a simple life, working hard in the fields throughout the year. As well as working on their own land, they also had to work for nothing on the thane's land.

(above) Anglo-Saxon noblemen were called **thanes**. To be a thane, a man had to own enough land to feed five families. The thanes were the king's chief warriors and they fought beside him in battle. The most important thanes helped the king by giving him advice. This was known as the **Witan**.

(above) The people who were unfree were called **slaves**. They had to perform the worst jobs, such as digging ditches, muck-spreading and tree cutting. In return for doing these jobs, they were given small gifts such as a pig, or gifts of food at Christmas.

In 1042, Edward the Confessor, the son of Ethelred the Unready, became king. Edward was a weak king and he had no sons to succeed him on the English throne. His right-hand man was Harold of Wessex, the most powerful thane in England. He was the man most likely to succeed King Edward.

Key
■ The Danelaw

STRATHCLYDE

NORTHUMBRIA

GWYNEDD

POWYS

MERCIA

DYFED

WESSEX

0   100m
0   160k

What do you say, merchant?
I go out with my ship ... and sell goods and buy costly things such as are not to be found in this country.
What sort of things do you bring across the sea?
Purple cloaks, silk, rare garments, herbs and spices, wine, oil, ivory ... and many other things besides.

B A merchant answers questions in *A Discussion on Work,* written by Aelfric around 1005

C A map showing the kingdoms of Wessex, Mercia and Northumbria before they were united by Alfred the Great. Also shown is the Danelaw, where the Vikings were allowed to settle after their invasion

1 **What were the main differences between churls and thralls?**

2 (a) **Read source B. In what way does this suggest that England was a rich country?**
   (b) **Who were likely to buy the goods brought into the country?**
   (c) **Who were unlikely to buy these goods?**

3 **How united was England by 1066? Were there any groups of people who might not have liked Anglo-Saxon control?**

4 **Look at the sources and the information in this chapter. Write a list under two headings;**
   (i) **similarities;**
   (ii) **differences**
   between Wales and England.
   Use this list as the basis for a piece of extended writing, headed 'The similarities and differences between Wales and England in the year 1000.'

2 The Norman conquest of England

Both the Welsh and the English were used to the invasions of the Vikings. But the Norman **invasion** was different. The Normans were more powerful and ambitious.

Who were the Normans?

The Normans were related to the Vikings. The Vikings had invaded France in the tenth century as part of the Viking invasions. They caused so much destruction that in the year 911, the King of France gave their leader, Rollo, a part of northern France. Because they came from the northern parts of Europe, these Vikings were called Normans and their land came to be known as Normandy. Rollo became the first Duke of Normandy.

Why were the Normans such good soldiers?

The secret of the Normans' power was the fact that that their horses were fitted with stirrups. This meant that the Norman soldiers could use their weapons with great effect against the enemy, without falling off their horses. In source A, Norman knights are riding into battle. You can easily pick out their uniforms - they are wearing mailcoats with hoods, iron helmets and iron guards. The mailcoat, called 'hauberk', was made up of thousands of tiny iron ringlets. They are also carrying kite shaped shields and lances.

Why did the Normans come to England?

The Normans were very warlike and adventurous. They came to England in 1066 under their leader Duke William. At the beginning of 1066, the English King, Edward the Confessor, died. Since Edward had no sons to succeed him, Harold of Wessex, the most powerful **earl** in the country was declared king.

William decided to challenge Harold's right to the throne because he believed that he should have been made the King of England. William was related to Edward the Confessor. According to a Norman writer called William of Poitiers, who wrote about these events, Harold had sworn an oath two years previously that he would support William's claim to be king. The *Anglo-Saxon Chronicle* does not mention this event at all. In addition, William of Poitiers's account of the way Harold became king differs from that of the *Chronicle* (see source D).

However, there was also another man who claimed the throne. He was Harald Hardrada, King of the Danes. Harald argued that he had the best claim to the kingship because his grandfather, Cnut, had ruled England before Edward the Confessor's time.

A Norman knights in battle, as depicted in the Bayeaux Tapestry

... the wise ruler entrusted the realm to a man of high rank, to Harold himself.

B From the *Anglo-Saxon Chronicle*

Harold swore an oath of loyalty to William ... after Edward's death he would do everything he could to make sure William became King of England.

C William of Poitiers, a Norman writer who recorded events during the eleventh century

Harold, on the day Edward died, seized the throne with the help of his evil followers and thereby broke the oath that he had made to William.

D William of Poitiers

E (left) These cartoons show how each of the claimants to the English throne argued their case

1 Read source D.
  (a) In your opinion, whose side was William of Poitiers on?
  (b) What do you think is the reason for this?
  (c) Give one example where William is expressing an opinion and give one example where he is stating a fact.

2 Why do you think the *Anglo-Saxon Chronicle* does not mention Harold's visit to William of Normandy?

3 In groups, discuss who had the best claim to the throne. After discussing this topic, write about your conclusions.

Year of Norman campaigns	Areas conquered	Year of Norman campaigns	Areas conquered
1066		1068 (Welsh Marches)	→
1068 (Spring)		1069–70	
1068 (Summer)		1070	

```
0          100m
0          160k
```

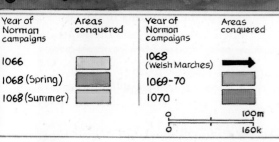

B Even after the Battle of Hastings, it took time for William to conquer the rest of England and Wales

The Battle of Hastings

In September 1066, Harald Hardrada landed on the north eastern coast of England with a large army. King Harold marched his army north to Stamford Bridge, where he met and defeated the Danes. In the meantime, William of Normandy had landed in Pevensey on the south coast of England. He had any army of 7,000 men, including 5,000 knights. Harold quickly returned to London and managed to raise a fresh army of soldiers.

The two armies met outside Hastings. The battle began early in the morning on 14 October 1066. At first, everything went in Harold's favour. He had the advantage of being situated at the top of a hill and his men were able to push back the Norman archers and foot soldiers whenever they charged towards them. Late in the afternoon, however, the Normans managed to trick the English by pretending to run away. When the English army ran down the hill, the Norman knights turned their horses around and, on the flat ground, they cut the English to pieces. Harold was killed in the struggle.

Some years after the battle, William's half-brother Odo, Bishop of Bayeux, ordered the whole story of how William became King of England to be illustrated in the form of a **tapestry**. This is known the Bayeux Tapestry. Source A is a section of the tapestry which shows the fiercest fighting at Hastings.

After the Battle of Hastings

It took the Normans only eight years to conquer the whole of England. The main reason for this was that most of England's bravest warriors were killed in the Battle of Hastings. Of those who survived, some left the country whilst others surrendered. But a few of them put up a brave fight against the Normans. They were put down with great cruelty by King William. In 1069, for example, a rebellion broke out in the north of England. The Normans dealt out harsh punishment for this (source C).

How did the feudal system work?

After he had conquered the English, William could do more or less what he liked. But at the same time, he had to do something to control his own men. The Normans had not fought alongside William for nothing. They expected to be rewarded.

William decided to pay them not in money but in land. (*Feudum* is a Latin word meaning land). Land was more valuable, at that time, than money. He gave parts of the land to his most important followers. He kept about a quarter of the territory he had conquered to himself. The rest of the country was shared out amongst the Norman earls and **barons**. They were called **Tenants in Chief** because they were given their lands directly from the king.

Every Tenant in Chief had to do homage to the king. He had to go on his knees and swear that he would be loyal to the monarch and be willing to fight for his ruler whenever he was called upon to do so, and to bring his knights with him at the same time.

This practice of sharing out land was then repeated at a lower level. The Tenant in Chief kept the best land to himself and shared the rest out amongst his own knights. They in turn had to fight for their lord whenever he wanted their service. This was a system designed for war.

At the lowest level of all, the ordinary people of England, both free and unfree, were forced to supply their Norman masters with food. They were allowed to keep their land, but they had to work on the lord of the manor's land for a set number of days per week. William was concerned that the lands of his most important barons were not bunched together in one place. He therefore scattered their territories (see source D).

The whole area around the town of York was burned to the ground: farm houses, animals and crops were completely destroyed. He searched through every inch of ground for the men whom he hated, and innocent people were also killed along with the guilty ones. He left such a shortage of food that the population of more than 100,000 people starved to death in the following year ...

C Orderic Vitalis

Key

Main lands held by Robert of Mortain

Other holdings

D (left) A map of England showing the way William scattered the lands of his important barons. Note the lands of Robert of Mortain

1 **What do each of these terms mean: Tenant in Chief; homage; Feudal System?**

2 **For what purpose was the Bayeux Tapestry made? List a few reasons.**

3 **Discuss in groups.**
   (a) What do you think were the advantages of the Feudal System?

(b) **Do you think that the Feudal System had any disadvantages for the King?**

(c) **Study source D. Why do you think that William scattered the lands of his chief followers through the length and breadth of England?**

4 **Read source C. Why do you think William was so cruel to the English?**

3 *T*he English conquest of Wales

(above) **A medieval illustration of a Welsh archer**

How did the Normans invade Wales?

The first Norman invasions of Wales lasted from 1067 until 1136. They were carried out by Norman barons. They captured large parts of Wales but they failed to take charge of the whole country. The Welsh often succeeded in pushing them back even from the areas that the Normans controlled. In the end, the King of England had to step in, but even he found it difficult.

The Normans entered Wales from three different points: Hugh of Avranches from Chester in the north, Roger of Montgomery from Shrewsbury in the centre and William Fitzosbern from Hereford in the south. In the share-out of land after 1066, these powerful barons had been given the territory between Wales and England. Their main task was to protect the borderland and, if possible, to extend it westward, into Wales. This meant that they could take as much territory as they liked. But they had to use their own private soldiers.

Mid and South Wales

At first, the Normans were unstoppable. Their foot soldiers and mounted knights could not be defeated on open, flat countryside. In 1067 William Fitzosbern of Hereford seized land in the kingdoms of Gwent and Brycheiniog (Brecon), and built castles at Chepstow and Monmouth. However, much of the hilly areas remained in Welsh hands.

In 1093 Rhys ap Tewdwr, King of Deheubarth, was killed outside

A Why did the Normans decide to invade Wales?

The possibility of gaining more land

The opportunity to serve the king

Becoming an even more powerful baron

A sense of adventure and a chance to continue fighting

The need to defend their own territory

Brecon fighting against Bernard of Neufmarché. Bernard went on to seize the rest of Brycheiniog. There was no one to take Rhys's place in South Wales, and during the years after 1093, there was nobody who could resist the Normans.

Robert Fitzhamon, Lord of Gloucester, conquered the Kingdom of Morgannwg (Glamorgan) and went on to build castles at Cardiff, Neath and Ogmore. Roger of Montgomery swept through central Wales and reached Cardigan and Pembroke. By 1100 much of the south-west of Wales had fallen into Norman hands. This area came to be known as the Welsh March. 'March' means frontier territory and the Norman barons who owned lands there were called the 'Lords of the March'.

North Wales

It was a different story in North Wales however. Gwynedd was ruled by a strong, ambitious king called Gruffudd ap Cynan (1081-1137). Hugh of Avranches, and his cousin Robert, almost succeeded in conquering Gwynedd. Robert got as far as Deganwy and built a castle at Rhuddlan, but was killed in 1087 causing the Normans to retreat.

However, the Normans' success in Wales did not last long. In 1135 a civil war broke out in England which lasted for almost twenty years until 1154. This meant the rulers of England could not give as much time to making sure Wales was under their control. The Welsh quickly struck back. In 1136 King Gruffudd ap Rhys of Deheubarth led a revolt against the Normans and before long they were being forced to retreat.

In the second half of the twelfth century, the Welsh cause was helped by two leaders: Owain Gwynedd in the north and Rhys ap Gruffudd in the south. From their bases in Aberffraw, in Anglesey and Dinefwr, in Deheubarth, they succeeded in defeating the Normans.

In 1154, Henry II became King of England. He brought the civil war to an end. But even he could not overcome the Welsh. In 1165 Henry II led a large expedition into Gwynedd. He never saw the Welsh forces because torrential rain forced him to return to England. In South Wales, Rhys ap Gruffudd was so powerful that Henry II decided make him the **overlord** of the whole of South Wales, giving him the title of Lord Rhys.

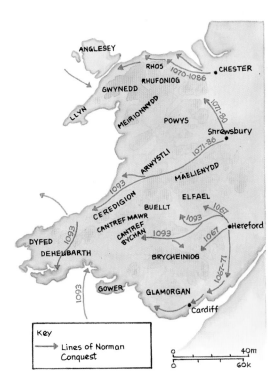

B A map of Wales showing the main campaigns made by the Normans

It is two hundred miles long and about one hundred miles wide. It takes some eight days to travel the whole length from the mouth of the River Gwygir in Anglesey to Portskewett in Gwent ... Because of its high mountains, deep valleys and extensive forests, not to mention its rivers and marshes, it is not easy of access.

C Gerald of Wales, in his *Description of Wales,* tells of the Welsh countryside

1 What might a Norman baron give as his reasons for invading Wales? Listing them in order, begin with the most important reason.

2 Study sources B and C. Why was Wales a difficult country to conquer?

3 Draw a timeline showing the Norman invasion of Wales.

4 Study the information in this chapter. Write an account entitled 'The Norman Invasions of Wales 1067-1200'. Use the following sub-headings:
 (i) How the Normans triumphed in Wales
 (ii) How the Welsh resisted the Normans

4 The English conquest of Wales: castles

> *The castle was not only a place of defence. It was also the headquarters of the government, containing the lord's office for running his affairs and for collecting rents and taxes.*

 A A description of the castle by the historian William Rees

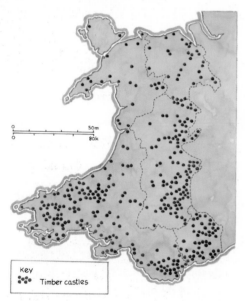

Key
●● Timber castles

Between 1075 and 1282, the Normans built a large number of castles in Wales. The castle gave them a huge advantage over the Welsh. They could use it as a means of both attack and defence. This was important to the Normans as they were few in numbers compared with the Welsh population.

The development of castles

The first castles built by the Normans were very rough-and-ready. They were called motte and bailey castles. They consisted of two main sections. The motte was a high mound, consisting of earth piled tightly together. The top of the mound was flattened and on it a wooden tower, called a keep, was built. This was surrounded by a circular wooden stockade. A bridge connected the motte to the bailey, which was the large area of ground surrounded by a wooden **palisade**. Deep ditches were dug around the motte and bailey. The ruins of those castles that are still standing today represent only a small proportion of the total number of castles built by the Normans in Wales.

The Normans, however, could never feel safe in their castles because the Welsh were always waiting for a chance to attack them.

B *(left)* **This map shows the distribution of timber castles across Wales in the eleventh and twelfth centuries**

C *(below)* **An illustration of a motte and bailey castle**

Motte (Mound)

Bailey (Enclosure)

Stockade (Fence)

Gerald of Wales, in his book *Journey Through Wales*, recounts an incident that took place 100 years previously, during the time of his grandfather, Gerald of Windsor. The year was 1096 when Welsh soldiers besieged Pembroke Castle. (See source E).

In order to make them more secure, the Normans had to change their castles. During the twelfth century, stone castles were built, usually alongside the old wooden ones. The circular wooden stockade was replaced by a stone wall, called a **curtain wall**. The entrance to the bailey was turned into a **barbican**, which was a tower over the gate. The wooden stockade on top of the mound was replaced with a stone wall which had **battlements**. The stone keep took the place of the wooden tower. This part of the castle came to be called the shell keep. Some of the keeps were square but later ones, built in the thirteenth century, were rounded. The wooden castles which were replaced by stone ones were those seen as the most important. These were located on good sites. Pembroke Castle, for example, was on excellent ground. As a result of these improvements special tactics and weapons were adopted to capture castles.

D A modern photograph of Pembroke Castle

When the defenders of the castle were almost close to starvation, Gerald of Windsor threw hog's meat over the walls. He then sent a letter to his friends saying that they could hold out for many more months and that help would not be needed. The letter was deliberately left at the Bishop's palace at St David's. When it was discovered, the content of the letter was made known to the besiegers, and as a result the Welsh army abandoned the siege of the castle.

E From *Journey Through Wales* by Gerald of Wales

---

1 (a) **Study source B. Where do most of these castles tend to be located? Why do you think there are so many of them?**

(b) **Study source C. What was the advantage of building the keep on top of the mound?**

2 **What advantages did the site of Pembroke Castle have?**

3 **Where in source D are the curtain walls and the barbican located?**

4 **Please work in groups. You and your fellow Welshmen are attacking Pembroke Castle. After discussing your tactics, write down your plan of campaign. Give reasons for your decisions.**

The Archbishop of Canterbury and other lords, as well as the princes of Wales, laid siege to the castle of Gwenwynwyn, King of Powys, at Welshpool. They used battering rams against the walls of the castle, but without success. In the end they tunnelled beneath the castle walls. The workmen who went underground were so skilful in undermining the moat and the mound that the people inside the castle were forced to surrender.

A The Chronicle of Wales recorded this incident in 1196

The construction of new castles

Other devices used (apart from those listed in source A) were siege catapults such as the mangonel and the trebuchet. It was in order to protect against such tactics that the **concentric castle** appeared during the thirteenth century. They were meant to be a foolproof method of defence.

These castles had two or three curtain walls instead of one. Among the first concentric castles to be built in Wales was Caerphilly Castle, built by the great Marcher Lord Gilbert de Clare between 1268 and 1281. Most of the other concentric castles were built on the orders of King Edward I after the final conquest of Wales in 1282. He built a series of them covering the whole of the old kingdom of Gwynedd. This included Flint, Rhuddlan, Conway, Beaumaris, Harlech and Caernarfon.

B A mangonel

C Beaumaris Castle seen from the air

---

1 Study source C. This is an aerial photograph. Why does this offer a better way of seeing the castle than a view seen from the ground?

2 (a) Put these changes in castle building in the order that they happened:
   (i) concentric castles;
   (ii) wooden motte and bailey castles;
   (iii) stone and shell keeps.
   For each change, explain why it happened.
   (b) In pairs, look at the picture of the stone castle on page 19 (opposite). Early wooden castles were very different from this stone one. Write down as many differences as you can think of. Compare your answers.

3 The historian D J Cathcart King, author of *Pembroke Castle*, has written as follows: 'Most of these colourful stories of the sieges were almost all imagined.'
   (a) Why do you think this historian doubts Gerald's story on page 17?
   (b) Does this make Gerald's description a worthless piece of historical information?

4 What does the number of concentric castles built in Wales tell you about the views of English rulers toward Wales?

8. This room was called the SOLAR, the baron's own private room

3. SPIRAL STAIRCASES were built enabling people to climb from one floor to the next. They were built clockwise, thereby putting right handed attackers at a disadvantage when swordfighting

10. In order to keep the draught out, the castle windows were small. There was no glass in the windows

1. THE GREAT HALL was the most important room in the castle. This room, usually taking up one floor of the castle keep, was where the main business of the castle was dealt with. It also served as the castle's main dining hall, and it was here also where most people slept. They wrapped themselves in blankets and slept on the floor

7. The rooms were dark and gloomy. Candles and rush lights provided the only light

4. This room was the baron's private CHAPEL, where both he and his family were served by a priest in services that were held every day

6. This picture shows servants carrying food to the great hall from the KITCHEN, located in a separate building from the castle keep

9. There were no carpets in the castle. The floor of the great hall, for example, was covered with rushes

2. This was the BASEMENT where the ales and wine were kept

5. This was the castle's toilets, called the GUARDROBE. These toilets were nothing more than stone seats covering a hole through which the sewage would run down the walls to the moat below

5 The English conquest of Wales: churches and monasteries

Once the Normans had built a castle in an area the next step was to build a church alongside it. The Church was very important to the Normans and it had a big part to play in their conquest of Wales.

The structure of the Church

The Church was very powerful in the Middle Ages and religion played a central role in society. Everybody had to be a Christian and everybody had to belong to a church. There was only one Church at that time - the Roman Catholic Church. At the head of the Catholic Church was the Pope who lived in Rome, Italy. The Church had influence all over Western Europe and in every country there was an archbishop to run the church on behalf of the Pope. Each country was divided into **dioceses**. A bishop was put in overall charge of each diocese. The bishop lived in a palace and his church was called a cathedral.

A The different members of the Church

The Pope

The Archbishop of Canterbury

Bishops

Priests

The ordinary people

Each diocese was made up of much smaller areas, called **parishes**, and in each parish there was a priest. It was the priest who looked after the needs of the ordinary people and it was he who forgave people for their wrongdoings. The better people were, the more likely they were to go to heaven. It was believed that in order to reach heaven, people had to attend church regularly on Sundays.

Maurice Londres, son of William de Londres, gave [land] to the church of St Peter's at Gloucester, the church of St Michael of Ewenny, the church of St Bride's Major with the Chapel of Ogmore ... and all their possessions ... in order that a convent of monks might be formed.

C From *The Chronicle of Gloucester*

The Church in Wales

The Normans organised Wales into four dioceses; St David's and Llandaff in South Wales, and Bangor and St Asaph in North Wales. The four bishops who were in charge of these dioceses had to take their orders from the leader of the Church in England, the Archbishop of Canterbury. He in turn was chosen by the King of England and appointed by the Pope. Wales was not allowed to have an archbishop of its own.

The Normans also built many churches in Wales. These churches were made of stone and they replaced the old Welsh wooden churches. The church shown in source B was built by the Norman knight William de Londres in 1116, soon after the conquest of the Kingdom of Morgannwg. His son also gave some of the land that William had conquered to the Church (source C). The Normans also tried to get rid of the old Welsh practice of allowing priests to marry. But this was difficult to stamp out.

A Welsh church has many people sharing in the living as there are important families living in the parish. When fathers die, the sons succeed, not by being elected, but as if they had inherited them, which is wrong in the sight of God. If a bishop dared to appoint anyone else, the people would take revenge on the man he chooses.

D Gerald, who wrote his book a 100 years after the Normans came to Wales, said this about the local churches

---

1 Why do you think that the top of the tower in source B is a similar shape to the top of a castle?

2 Why do think the Normans gave so much land to the Church?

3 Why do you think the Normans put their own men in charge of the Welsh Church?

4 Why were people so religious at that time?

5 What evidence is there in sources B and C to show that the Normans were religious?

6 What evidence is there that the Welsh were religious?

A
A twelfth-century monastery at
Strata Florida

Monasteries

As the Normans swept through Wales at the beginning of the twelfth century, they built not only churches but monasteries as well. They replaced the earlier monasteries of the Celtic Church with Benedictine monasteries. These monasteries followed the rules of St Benedict as laid down in the sixth century. They were known as Black Monks, named after their black coloured clothing. In Wales, the monasteries were built near Norman castles, including places such as Monmouth, Brecon and Carmarthen. Most of the monks who lived in them came from Normandy. As a result they were not popular with the Welsh people.

Later on, however, the Normans brought another type of monastic organisation into Wales called the Cistercian Order, founded in Burgundy, France, by St Bernard of Clairvaux. The idea behind it was to adhere more strictly to the rule of St Benedict. One of the first Cistercian monasteries in Wales was set up at Whitland by Bernard, the Bishop of St David's, in 1098. A branch of this monastery was established by a Norman knight, Robert Fitz Stephen, at Strata Florida on the lonely Cardiganshire moors. (Source A).

Cistercian houses were established in other parts of Wales at Tintern, Basingwerk and Aberconwy. They were popular with the Welsh people, particularly the Welsh kings. Lord Rhys gave generously to the Abbey of Strata Florida. Many Welsh rulers were buried there, as well as the famous Welsh poet Dafydd ap Gwilym. The Cistercians pioneered sheep farming. They wore white woollen clothes and became known as White Monks.

Each monastery followed the same basic plan. There was the church, forming the heart of the monastery, shaped in the form of a cross. Next to it was the cloister. This was a kind of gallery surrounding an open rectangular space. Around this space would be located rooms, such as the chapter house, the **dormitory** and the **refectory**.

Most of the monasteries in Wales were built between roughly 1200 and 1300. During this period, monks kept to the strict rules laid down by their orders. Later on, however, as the monastries became richer, they became more relaxed about these orders. Sources C, D, E, F and G give us an idea of what happened.

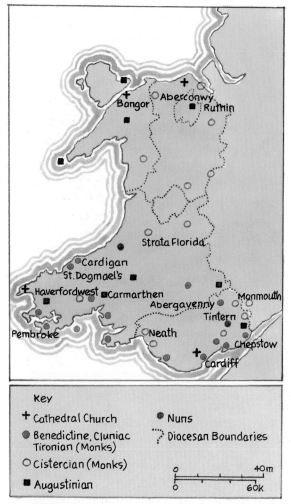

Key
+ Cathedral Church
● Benedictine, Cluniac Tironian (Monks)
○ Cistercian (Monks)
■ Augustinian
● Nuns
⋯ Diocesan Boundaries

0   40m
0   60k

B
A map showing the various types of monasteries in Wales

... great store of learning was brought together by Lanfranc in the abbey of Bec in Normandy ... the whole community is full of joy and charity in the service of God. I cannot speak too highly of the hospitality of Bec ... The doors of Bec are always open to any traveller ...

C
Orderic Vitalis's description of the Abbey of Bec in 1125

Vigils	Matins	Prime	Tierce	Sext	Nones	Vespers	Compline

2.0am	Prayers in the abbey church	12.0noon	Main dinner eaten in the refectory
3.0am	Back to bed in the dormitory	12.30pm	Prayers in the abbey church
6.0am	Get up at sunrise Prayers in the abbey church Breakfast of bread and ale in the refectory	1.0pm	Work at the farm or mill
		6.0pm	Prayers in the abbey church
7.0am	Meeting in the chapter house to organise work for the day	7.0pm	Supper in the refectory
8.0am	Walk in the cloisters to relax and think	8.0pm	Prayers in the abbey church
11.0am	Prayers in the abbey church	9.0pm	Bedtime in the dormitory

F A monk's daily duties

1401. We found among other things that some of the monks of your said house bring into their cells private persons from outside, entertaining them … and they live loosely, going out of bounds without the leave of the prior.

D Visitation of the Bishop of St David's to the Abbey of Carmarthen in 1401

In 1401-2 where there used to be a full convent of honest monks, there are now only three of them left … And we urge you that none of the monks are allowed to visit any tavern or to engage in heavy drinking in the town of St Dogmaels.

E Visitation of the Bishop of St David's to the Abbey of St Dogmael

The religious Orders had passed their peak by 1300. The quality of monastic life tended to change for the worse – no new monasteries were founded in Wales after that … and abbots, on whom the standard of life within the monastery depended, often built fine houses for themselves.

G Glanmor Williams: *Monuments of Conquest: Castles and Cloisters* (1973)

1 In what ways did monasteries change for the worse during the Middle Ages?

2 (a) In what ways were Benedictine monks similar to Cistercian monks?
   (b) In what ways were the two types of monks different from each other?

3 (a) Look at the map of Wales (source B). Why do you think that Benedictine monasteries tended to be located in South Wales?
   (b) What do you notice about the location of Cistercian monasteries?

4 Describe in detail a day in the life of a monk at Strata Florida Abbey.

5 The Middle Ages have been described as a golden age in the history of the Christian Church. On the basis of this chapter, write an essay supporting this description. (You must make full use of the information found in this chapter).

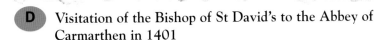

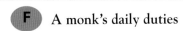

6 The English conquest of Wales: towns

Each burgess has to pay an annual rent of twelve pence for each service.
Each burgess can sell his property to whomsoever he pleases.
Each burgess can give his son or daughter in marriage without having to get anyone's permission.
Each one can sell his oxen, his horse and any other goods without having to ask the Lord for permission.
Also, each burgess can brew and bake without a licence, and without having to pay tolls.

A Extracts from the Charter of Cardiff

Walter Hereford	*John Porter*
Reginald Carewell	*John Maniers*
John Skiret	*Philip Carpenter*
Walter Narber	*Julian Taylor*
Simon Montefort	*William Blida*
Jacob Cestria	*Marione Mauncel*

B Some burgesses of Caernarfon

Robert Sayer	*Stephen Cras*
William Plumer	*David Grug*
Ieuan ap Vychan	*John de Turri*
ap Ieuan ap Rhys	*Adam ap Gronw*
Walter ap Thomas	

C Some burgesses of Aberystwyth

Since there were no proper towns in Wales before the coming of the Normans, the Marcher Lords built castles, and towns often grew up around these in order to supply the Marcher Lord, his family and his soldiers. Some of their needs were:

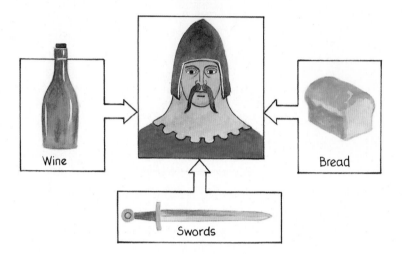

Can you think of any other needs?

Products were provided by French and English immigrants who were persuaded to settle in these new towns. They were called **burgesses** and the towns which they inhabited were called boroughs. They were given special privileges that were recorded in a document called the town charter. These town charters were pioneered by William Fitzosbern, who based them on the charter of the town of Breteuil in Normandy. The Charter of Cardiff (source A) gives you an idea of what the Marcher Lord had to offer.

Later on, new boroughs were set up by the Kings of England. Henry I, for example, brought Flemish settlers into south Pembrokeshire and, after the final conquest of Wales, Edward I allowed English immigrants into the boroughs set up by him in North Wales. Sources B and C list of the some of the burgesses of Caernarfon and Aberystwyth in 1298.

Edward I also declared that the towns were built to be initially peopled by English settlers. He also insisted that no one living within five miles of any borough in Wales could buy or sell goods. This meant that the Welsh had no choice but to sell their goods in the royal boroughs where they had to pay heavy tolls.

After the Glyndŵr Rebellion (1399-1412), these rules became even stricter. They were called the Penal Laws. An example of one of these laws is given in source D.

No Welsh person from now on can buy lands or dwellings in any of the Boroughs or Commercial Towns of Wales.

F A fourteenth-century illustration of a French town square

D One of the Penal Laws passed after the Glyndŵr Rebellion

Bath, Worcester, Chester, Hereford: Do not select your home in the northern cities, nor in Worcester, Hereford or Chester, because of the desperate Welshmen

E Advice given, as a result of the Penal Laws, by Richard of Devizes in his *Chronicles of the Crusades*

1 (a) Look at the list of names in source B. What do you think the attitude of the Welsh would have been to this list?
  (b) In what way does the list from Aberystwyth in source C contradict Edward I's ruling?

2 Why do you think that both English and French people were prepared to settle in Wales?

3 Source F comes from France. In what way is it relevant to our understanding of life in Welsh towns during the Middle Ages?

4 Why did Norman and, later, English rulers not want Welsh people to live in these towns? Give reasons for your answer.

5 What do you think the views of Welsh people were toward the towns?

7 Henry II and Thomas Becket

A Henry I's nightmare

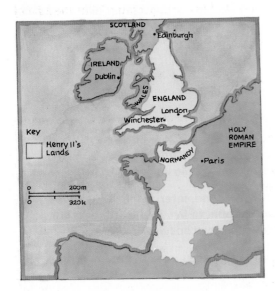

B A map of Henry II's empire in 1154

Source A shows Henry I (1100-1135), having a bad dream with peasants, barons and bishops, ganging up on him. This nightmare actually became reality. For 14 years, from 1139 to 1153, England was plunged into civil war between Stephen, Henry's nephew, and Matilda, his daughter. The war ended with the coming to the throne of Matilda's son, Henry II. Henry was determined to unite the country and bring back law and order.

Henry II was strong, clever, energetic and ambitious. He ruled a vast **empire**. Not only was he King of England and Normandy, he also ruled large areas of France and claimed to be ruler of Wales and Ireland.

Henry succeeded in making his barons, both in England and France, respect him. He did this by visiting every part of his kingdom. This required a great deal of travelling. For the 32 years of his reign, Henry crossed the English Channel 28 times (this was not easy in the Medieval period). Illegal castles which had been built during the civil war were pulled down and royal lands, lost during the conflict, were recovered. New taxes were imposed and collected by the royal sheriffs.

Henry also sent royal judges to every district in England to make sure that the law was upheld fairly. These travelling judges were called Justices in Eyre. Through two announcements, the Assize of Clarendon (1166) and the Assize of Northampton (1176), Henry also developed the idea of a jury system, which meant that twelve men were able to take part in the judgement of legal cases. The king's written orders, called the Royal Writ, began to be respected throughout the country. As a result, people began to prefer the king's courts to the barons' courts.

Once he had controlled the barons, Henry next turned his attention to the Church, the other main source of power in his realm. In 1161 the Archbishop of Canterbury, the head of the English Church, died. In his place, Henry appointed his best friend and Chancellor, Thomas Becket. Henry was determined to control the Church. He thought that Becket would do the job for him. Henry was particularly concerned about the church courts, where anyone with connections received lighter sentences than they would have in the king's courts.

Once he started in his new post, however, Thomas Becket began to behave independently. Becket became very religious and disobeyed Henry's orders. In 1164 the king announced that churchmen who had been found guilty in the church courts could be sentenced a second time in the king's courts. But Becket refused to obey Henry's ruling. Henry was furious and the two men quarrelled. In 1170 things got worse when Becket expelled two bishops from the church. They had crowned the king's son when Becket was out of the country.

Four knights (see source E) travelled to Canterbury and murdered Becket on the altar of the cathedral. By murdering Thomas Becket, Henry failed to get complete control of the Church. He continued to appoint bishops, but he failed to stop Church courts from putting churchmen, who had broken the law, on trial. Becket was made a saint and Henry was forced to walk barefoot to Canterbury to show that he was sorry.

Things were never the same afterwards. The clash between Becket and the king damaged Henry's earlier successful work in controlling the barons. During the last 15 years of his life, Henry was at odds with his four sons. They disagreed with the way that their father intended to share out his empire on his death. They were backed up by the King of France. Twice they rose in open war against their father. Henry died an unhappy man. His empire was intact but he left many problems for his successors to cope with.

D Thomas Becket leaves Henry I. An illustration from a medieval manuscript which told the story of Becket's life

He was chosen by God

He was responsible for law and order

Officially the owner of all the land

He made all the big decisions

The barons had to fight in his army

He selected people for the top jobs

C The king's powers

'My lord, while Thomas lives you will not have peace and quiet' … Henry lost his temper completely. Seeing this, four knights of his household who were eager to win the king's favour met together and swore to arrange the archbishop's death.

E This is an account from the *Life of Thomas Becket* by William Fitz Stephen, of one bishop's words to Henry, and the resulting conspiracy

1 Give one long-term reason and one short-term reason for the murder of Thomas Becket.

2 Why do you think Becket behaved differently once he was made Archbishop of Canterbury?

3 Give two consequences of the murder of Thomas Becket.

4 Discuss in groups the murder of Becket. One member should take on Henry II's role, another member Becket's role. The others must question both characters in order to discover whether Henry II should take all of the blame for the murder.

5 'The Head of the Church in England was bound to clash with the King of England.' Do you agree with this statement? If so why? (Chapter 5 will provide you with additional information).

8 The Crusades

A A fifteenth-century painting of Jerusalem

The Turks have overrun your brothers, slaughtering and capturing many and destroying churches. They cut open their navels, and tear out their insides. They tie them to a stake, or drag them and flog them. All men going there who die will immediately be forgiven for their sins.

B Part of Pope Urban II's speech in 1095

The Welsh fought regularly against the Normans. But sometimes they were willing to forget their differences and to fight alongside one another. This was especially true of the Crusades - the great campaign to defend the city of Jerusalem from the Turks. At that time, every Christian believed that Jerusalem was the most important place in the whole world.

Jerusalem was called the Holy City because it was there that Jesus Christ had been crucified. The city was situated in the Holy Land. The Holy Land was under the control of the Arab people. They believed in the same God as Christians but followed the teachings of their own religious leader, called Muhammed, who had lived during the sixth century. The followers of Muhammed were called Muhammedans or Muslims. At first there was peace between the Christians and the Muslims. However, in the eleventh century, a group of warlike people, called the Turks, took control of the Holy Land from the Arabs. They too followed the religion of Muhammed, but they were more strict in their beliefs than the Arabs. They made it more difficult for Christians to travel to Jerusalem. Many Christian pilgrims travelling through the Holy Land were killed by the Turks.

In 1095 the Pope condemned the Turks and appealed to the Christian peoples of Europe to drive them out of the Holy City of Jerusalem (source B). He told them that God would reward those who fought on behalf of Jesus Christ. Almost 10,000 people, from all over Europe, responded to the call.

By 1099 the main crusading army had reached Jerusalem. The Turks defended the city well and the crusaders had to spend the

C (below) A map of Europe showing the routes taken to the Holy Land by Richard I, Philip II and Fredrick Barbarossa

Key
- ••••• Frederick Barbarossa's route -1190
- •••• Richard 1's route -sailed from Marseilles
- —— Philip II's route- sailed from Genoa

0 ————— 500m
0 ————— 800k

North Sea
Baltic Sea
London
Boulogne   GERMANY
Paris
RUSSIA
Caspian Sea
Vienna
WESTERN EMPIRE   HUNGARY
Venice   Black Sea
Marseilles   Genoa
Rome   Constantinople
Adriatic Sea
ANATOLIA   Edessa   Mosul
Athens   Aleppo   Baghdad
GREECE   CYPRUS   Antioch
RHODES   Tripoli
CRETE   Tyre
Acre
Jerusalem
Atlantic Ocean
Mediterranean Sea
Cairo   Damietta

whole of the summer trying to capture it. After a fierce fight, the crusaders succeeded in taking the city but many men, from both sides, were killed horribly.

Jerusalem was now in Christian hands. Nevertheless, the Christians were not allowed to live in peace. The Turks fought back and in 1147 a Second Crusade was organised but this failed completely. Then, in 1187, a fierce Muslim leader appeared called Salah al-Din, who was called Saladin by the Europeans. He defeated a Christian army in 1187 and, in the same year, he recaptured the city of Jerusalem.

This event shocked the whole of Europe. The new Pope called for another crusade against the Muslims. This time, there was a stronger response to his appeal. Three of the most powerful kings in Europe came forward - Richard I (King of England), Philip II (King of France) and Fredrick Barbarossa (the Emperor of Germany). The Archbishop of Canterbury travelled the length and breadth of Wales, preaching about the crusade, accompanied by Gerald of Wales. (This was the main reason for Gerald's journey which you learned about at the beginning of the book.) Gerald wrote a vivid account of this recruitment drive called *Journey Through Wales*.

Over 3,000 Welshmen, according to Gerald, went on the Third Crusade. Only a few them actually reached the Holy Land. This was typical of many crusaders. Fredrick Barbarossa, for example, was drowned whilst travelling through Turkey. Philip II and Richard I travelled by sea to the Holy Land.

E A thirteenth-century crusading knight

A sermon was given at Abergavenny and many took the Cross. A certain nobleman of those parts, called Arthenus ... took the Cross from the Archbishop without waiting any longer.
In Usk Castle a large group of men was signed with the Cross ... some of the most notorious criminals of those parts were among those converted, robbers, highwaymen and murderers. Twelve archers from the castle of St Clears, murdered a young Welshman, and on the following day were signed with the Cross as a punishment for the crime.

D All sorts of people joined in the crusade. An extract from Gerald's *Journey Through Wales*

Nearly the whole city was crammed with bodies. The Saracens who were still alive dragged the dead ones out in front of the gates and made huge piles of them, as big as houses ...

F From the *Gesta Francorum*

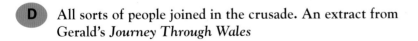

1 Look at source A. How does the artist convey to us the idea that Jerusalem was a holy city?

2 Working in pairs:
   (a) Read sources B and D. Make a list of all the different types of people who joined the Crusades. Discuss with your partner why they were willing to join the Crusades.

   (b) Make a list of all the countries that are mentioned in this section. What other countries would have been likely to support the crusaders?

3 (a) How do you know that the knight in source E is a crusader?
   (b) Draw a time line of the First, Second and Third Crusades.

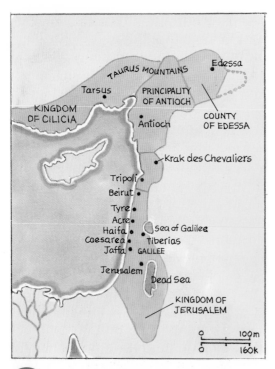

A A map showing the crusader lands, captured by 1186

Two thousand seven hundred Muslims, all in chains, were led outside the wall, where they were slaughtered every one. We thank God for this!

B Ambroise, a French Christian, gave his views

C A picture showing human heads being thrown into a city using giant catapults

The fighting

When Richard I and Philip II reached the Holy Land in 1191, they had to seize the city of Acre on the coast. Acre had been under siege for two years. They took two months to capture it. Philip II then became ill and had to return home to France. However, Richard led his army south to meet and defeat the forces of Saladin, at Arsuf. When he reached Jerusalem, Richard realized that his army was not big enough to take the city. A ceasefire was agreed upon and the English king went back to England. The Third Crusade came to an end.

There were four more crusades to the Holy Land but not one of them succeeded in recapturing Jerusalem. The crusaders caused a great deal of suffering and cruelty, sometimes long before they reached the Holy Land. We have written and visual evidence of the violence of the crusaders. (See sources B,C and E).

The effects of the Crusades

A historian has to decide the extent to which events have an effect upon people. This is not at all easy. In the case of the Crusades, the historian has to look at all of them over a long period of time, and try to measure the changes that were brought into Europe as a result.

The Crusades increased the contacts between Europe and the East. This contact took the form of buying and selling goods. During the periods of peace in between the Crusades, the Europeans learned a great deal about the Muslims. They learned, for example, that just as Europeans had different languages and customs, so the Muslims had theirs. They learned to appreciate the knowledge that the Arabs had. They knew more than the Europeans did about mathematics, science and medicine. The Europeans began to **import** goods such as silk, gold, iron, soap and glass.

D An illustration of a crusader playing chess with a Muslim

The Crusades also had a big influence on castle building in Europe. Edward I, for example, went to the Holy Land and saw for himself the powerful castles built by the crusaders who had copied them from the Muslims. These castles influenced the design of the huge castles that he built in Wales. Yet, in spite of these contacts, the Europeans still regarded the Arabs with suspicion.

> They brought out the Muslim prisoners. God had decided that they would become martyrs that day. More than three thousand were tied together with ropes and then killed. The Franks rushed at them all at once and slaughtered them in cold blood.

E   The event described in source B was written about by a Muslim supporter of Saladin

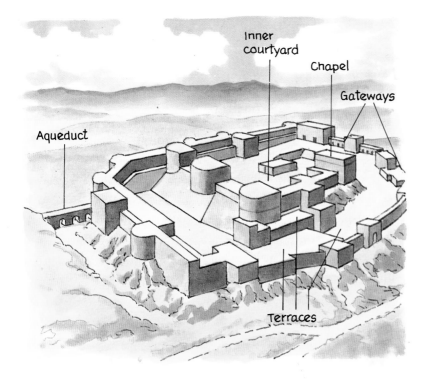

F   Plans of the Crusader Castle, Krak des Chevaliers, in Syria

> ... the Christians captured large hoards of Muslim coins in Palestine, Spain and Sicily. As a result, princes became wealthy and bought from merchants, the luxury goods imported from the east...

G   David Nicholas: *The Evolution of the Medieval World*

Not all historians agree on the effects of the Crusades

> *Writer after writer repeated old lies about Muhammed, that he was an epileptic, that he smeared himself with lipstick and drenched himself in perfume. He was called 'the deceiver' and even 'the Devil' himself.*

H   An extract from *A Letter to Christendom* by Rana Kabbani

> *There is no doubt that the Crusades ... hastened the development of commerce in Europe.*

I   D J Geanakoplos: *Western Civilization*

> *The Crusades have been credited with reviving trade between east and west, but such claims are exaggerated.*

J   David Nicholas: *The Evolution of the Medieval World*

---

1 (a) **Read sources B and E. In what way does source E agree with source B?**
  (b) **What additional item of information is given by source E?**
  (c) **Which source is the most reliable in your opinion? (Clue: look at the authors.)**

2 (a) **Make a list of the effects that the Crusades had upon Europe. Who benefited, do you think, from these changes?**
  (b) **Who do you think did not benefit from these changes?**

3 **Why do you think it is difficult for historians to agree about the effects of the Crusades on life in Europe?**

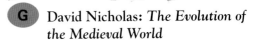

9 King John and the Magna Carta

Source A is a nineteenth-century painting of King John sealing the Magna Carta. This is a Latin phrase meaning Great Charter and John signed it towards the end of his reign in 1215, at Runnymede, an island in the middle of the River Thames. John's big mistakes were his military failures and his quarrels with the barons and the Church.

Soon after becoming king, John was fighting a war which broke out between England and France. By 1204, John had lost all the King of England's territories in northern France, including Normandy. He spent the rest of his reign trying to get them back, during the course of which he quarrelled with the big barons of England.

John had to have a large army in order to invade France. The money needed to pay for it had to come from extra taxes. It was these heavy taxes which angered the barons, especially those who received no favours from him in return.

John also had the reputation for being a cruel man. In 1200 it was said that he had his fifteen-year-old nephew, Arthur, murdered. In 1208, when one of the Welsh Marcher Lords, called William de Braose, fell out with him, he had de Braose's wife and son thrown into prison where they were left to starve to death.

To cap it all, John also clashed with the Church. In 1205 the Archbishop of Canterbury died. John wanted his own man to be archbishop. But the Pope in Rome, Innocent III, wanted Stephen Langton to have the post. John refused to co-operate. He took over all of the Church's property in England. In 1208, Pope Innocent **excommunicated** John and imposed an **interdict** on England. This meant that no services were to be held on Sundays and that the churches would be shut. This caused much unhappiness.

In 1213 the Pope persuaded Philip, King of France, to invade England since neither John nor the English people belonged to the Catholic Church any longer. But at the last minute, John surrendered. He agreed to allow Stephen Langton to become Archbishop of Canterbury and apologised to Pope Innocent for the trouble he had caused.

In 1214, the French army defeated the Emperor Otto IV, one of John's allies, at Bouvines. This was the last straw. The barons rose in rebellion against John. As a result the Magna Carta was sealed by him in June 1215.

John died in 1216. But the terms of Magna Carta were to stay. During the reign of John's son Henry III (1216-72), the barons forced Henry to call the first **Parliament** in the history of England. During the reigns of subsequent kings, Parliament became more and more important.

A An artist's impression of John at Runnymede

B Prisoners being tortured

Was John a bad king?

You can see from this account that John has gone down in history as a thoroughly bad man. This is largely based on descriptions that have come down to us from that time. Sources C, D, and E provide us with conflicting views.

Loyalty to man, law or God, meant nothing to him (John).

C Prévite-Orton: *The Cambridge History of the Middle Ages* (1952)

The chancery records clearly show that John took an active interest in the day to day details of governing the country ... he was not idle ... John was no coward ... he had a genuine interest in the legal system.

D A L Poole: *Domesday Book to Magna Carta* (1964)

In a temper John would gnash his teeth and roll his straining eyes in fury. Then he would sometimes pick up sticks and straws and gnaw them like a madman and sometimes he would cast them away half chewed.

E Matthew of Paris, a monk who lived between 1200 and 1259 gave this description of John

No new taxes without agreement

Towns should keep their privileges

No freeman to be imprisoned without a trial

No interference with the Church

Heirs to inherit without interference

Widows will inherit without interference

Merchants to be able to travel freely

25 barons will make sure these promises are not broken

F A modern illustration showing the terms of the Magna Carta

1 (a) **Study the terms of the Magna Carta as shown in source F. What groups of people were affected by each one? State the reasons why you think this is so.**
   (b) **Which terms of the agreement affected everyone in the country?**

2 **Why do you think the loss of Normandy was bad news for the rulers of Wales, Scotland and Ireland?**

3 **Use all the information to be found in this chapter to answer the following question: Was John a bad king?**

*T*he age of the two Llywelyns, 1194-1282

A An artist's impression of Dafydd ap Llywelyn being acknowledged as the rightful heir to his father's kingdom

B *(below & right)* Llywelyn and his policies

The reign of Llywelyn the Great 1194-1240

Llywelyn the Great was the first Welsh king who united Wales against the Norman invaders. He was the Prince of Gwynedd between 1194 and 1240. Gwynedd was Wales's most powerful kingdom. Its high and rugged mountains gave it protection during times of trouble. At such times, the people of Gwynedd could be supplied with food from the island of Anglesey.

Llywelyn had seized Gwynedd from his cousins. In order to turn it into a powerful kingdom, Llywelyn had copied the methods, used by William the Conqueror, to make England stronger. (Source B summarises what he did).

Llywelyn then set about seizing the rest of Wales. Powys and Deheubarth, at that time, were ruled by weak kings. He easily imposed himself upon them. In 1216 the rulers of Deheubarth went to Aberdyfi to accept Llywelyn's ruling as to the way their lands should be divided.

Llywelyn and the Lords of the March

If Llywelyn was serious about uniting the whole of Wales, he knew that he had to defeat the Lords of the March. They controlled about half of the entire country. The first big Norman baron he quarrelled with was William Marshall, the Lord of Pembroke. The quarrel was sparked off in 1220 when Llywelyn complained that Marshall's men

He built stone castles such as Dolbadarn Castle and Castell-y-Bere

He appointed Welshmen to important positions in the Church

He raised taxes

He formed a council of able men to run the country

were trying to steal the land and cattle of his Welsh subjects. Llywelyn invaded Dyfed in 1220. He destroyed two castles and set the town of Haverfordwest on fire (see source C). In 1223, William Marshall struck back and recaptured the castles of Carmarthen and Cardigan.

Llywelyn also fought against another powerful Marcher Lord, William de Braose. In 1228, de Braose was captured and was forced to pay Llywelyn for his release. However, in 1230, Llywelyn discovered that his wife Joan had been having an affair with de Braose. As a result de Braose was hanged and Joan was forced to watch his execution.

Llywelyn and the Kings of England

Between 1199 and 1216 England was ruled by King John. John felt that Llywelyn was getting too powerful and so decided to teach him a lesson. In 1211, John invaded Wales and defeated Llywelyn. By this time, however, John had his own problems with his barons back in England.

After John's death, Llywelyn signed a peace treaty with John's son Henry III at Worcester. According to this treaty, Llywelyn was allowed to keep all the lands that he had won and he was recognised as the main ruler of Wales.

Could Wales be permanently united?

Llywelyn was determined to keep Wales united after his death. He had two sons, Dafydd and Gruffudd. The laws of Wales stated that Gwynedd would have to be divided between them. But Llywelyn insisted that it should be passed on to Dafydd. Gruffudd strongly disagreed with this and Llywelyn had him put into prison. In 1238, Llywelyn called another meeting of the rulers of Wales at Strata Florida. There he had them swear an oath of loyalty to Dafydd. (See source A.)

> Whilst William Marshall was in Ireland, Llywelyn, the King of Wales, seized two castles and he cut off the heads of everyone that was found inside them, and then he left these castles in the hands of his Welsh followers.

C Roger of Wendover, a monk living at St Albans, described the clash between Llywelyn and William Marshall

> In that year, William Marshall came to Deheubarth with a large navy and a host of knights and foot soldiers from Ireland; and he landed at St David's during Palm Sunday. And then on Good Friday, and without any warning, the castle was forced to surrender. And when Llywelyn heard this, he sent his son Gruffydd with a large number of men against the earl; because these castles had been given to Llywelyn by the King.

D The event written about in source C, was also recorded in the *Chronicle of the Princes*

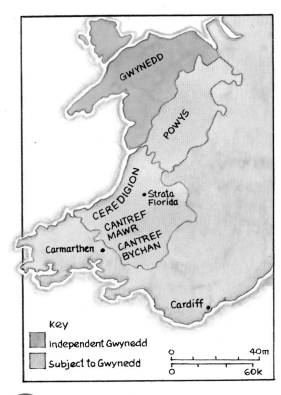

key

▢ Independent Gwynedd

▢ Subject to Gwynedd

E A map of Wales in 1237

---

1 Draw a timeline of the main events in the reign of Llywelyn the Great.

2 (a) In what ways are sources C and D similar to each other?
   (b) In what ways are they different from each other?

3 In what way does source D favour Llywelyn? What are the reasons for this?

4 Look at source A. Who are the people taking part in this ceremony? Who are 1, 2, 3 and 4?

5 Look at source E. What did Dafydd need to do once he became king?

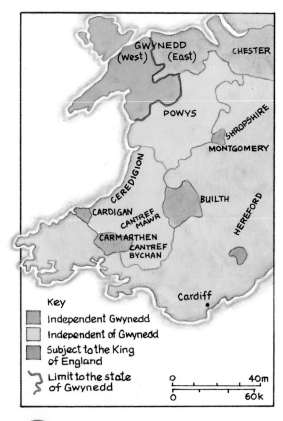

A A map of Wales in 1247

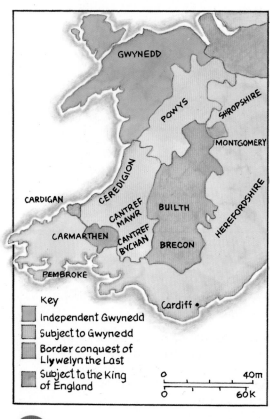

B A map of Wales in 1267

Dafydd ap Llywelyn loses everything

Dafydd ap Llywelyn's reign lasted for only six years, from 1240 until 1246. He failed to keep the Welsh rulers behind him. They supported his brother Gruffudd. Henry III took advantage of these quarrels and took Gruffudd prisoner. However, in 1244 Gruffudd was killed whilst trying to escape from the Tower of London and in 1247, Henry III invaded Gwynedd. The kingdom was cut down to size. (Source A shows the lands that were taken by Henry).

After 1247 the Welsh were hemmed in by the English. Henry III controlled a string of castles around Gwynedd and the other Welsh rulers had to swear an oath of loyalty to him. Henry was also backed up by the Marcher Lords. It seemed only a matter of time before the rest of Wales would fall into the hands of the English.

However, during the next thirty years, the men of Gwynedd struck back. Their leader was Llywelyn ap Gruffudd. He made himself the sole ruler of Gwynedd and forced Powys and Deheubarth to swear loyalty to him rather than to Henry III. In 1258, Llywelyn adopted the title of Prince of Wales.

Henry III wanted to teach Llywelyn a lesson. But he was prevented from doing so because the chief barons of England rebelled against him, under the leadership of Simon de Montfort. In 1265, Llywelyn teamed up with Simon de Montfort and married his daughter. In 1267, Henry signed a new treaty with Llywelyn at Montgomery. This is what the Treaty of Montgomery said:

1) Henry recognised Llywelyn as the Prince of Wales.
2) Llywelyn was allowed to speak on behalf of the rulers of Wales and paid Henry a sum of money.
3) Henry had to return to Llywelyn all the lands that he had taken from him in 1247.

Gwynedd was now much larger and stronger. Llywelyn seemed to be on the point of uniting Wales as Llywelyn the Great had done.

Llywelyn ap Gruffudd and Edward I

Henry III died in 1272. He was replaced by his son Edward I. Edward was a more powerful personality than his father. He was determined to make himself the master of the whole of Britain. Wales was the first country on his list. Unlike his father, Edward succeeded in rallying the lords behind him, including the Lords of the March. The Marcher Lords were afraid that Llywelyn would seize their lands. In 1268, Llywelyn had demolished a castle that Gilbert de Clare was building at Caerphilly, and so de Clare had had to build an even bigger castle there.

Another big advantage that Edward had over Llywelyn was that he was able to exploit Llywelyn's quarrels with other Welsh rulers. Llywelyn was taking on the airs and graces of a king of the whole of Wales, which they disliked intensely. In 1274, one of these rulers, Gruffudd ap Gwenwynwyn of Powys, with the help of Llywelyn's brother Dafydd ap Gruffudd, plotted to assassinate Llywelyn. The plot failed and Dafydd fled for safety to England.

Llywelyn felt that he was on an equal footing with Edward I. He failed to appear at Edward I's coronation, and refused to pay homage to him. Edward ordered Llywelyn to do so five times between 1274 and 1276, and on each occasion Llywelyn refused. Edward got fed up with this. In 1277 Edward I declared war on Llywelyn and invaded Wales.

C This picture shows Llywelyn ap Gruffudd of Wales (1) and Alexander III of Scotland (2) attending one of Edward I's Parliaments. This is an imaginary scene painted in 1534, over 250 years after the reign of Edward I (3)

1 Compare the maps in sources A and B. In what ways are they similar to each other? In what way are they different from each other?

2 Why do you think the rulers of Powys and Deheubarth resented Dafydd ap Llywelyn and Llywelyn ap Gruffudd?

3 (a) Look at source C. What idea is the artist trying to create in this scene?

(b) In what way can source C give the wrong impression of what actually happened during the reign of Edward I?

4 In the quarrel between Llywelyn ap Gruffudd and Edward I, who do you think was in the right? Were they both right? Give reasons for your choice.

How did Llywelyn die?

> And then, in the belfry of Bangor cathedral, Llywelyn was betrayed by his own men.

A *The Chronicle of Princes*

> Beyond the river Wye, the King's men were encamped under Lord Giffard and Lord Mortimer. Then Llywelyn was spotted by one of our soldiers, Stephen de Frankton. De Frankton and some soldiers went after him ... although he did not know who he was. He killed him with his lance. It was only afterwards that Llywelyn's body was identified.

B Walter of Guisborough also described Llywelyn's death

> Lord Roger Mortimer had been plotting to kill Llywelyn through trickery. When Llywelyn's men reached the spot, his enemies attacked him and killed him.

C *The Hagnaby Chronicle*

> It is known that the person who was present at Llywelyn's death found a letter of betrayal under a false name hidden on his body.

D From a letter sent by Archbishop Pecham to Edward I

Llywelyn's final defeat

The war of 1277 was over within a few months. (Source E shows how Edward defeated Llywelyn.)

1) Gwynedd was now surrounded by territories under Edward I's control.
2) New castles were built or refortified, such as Rhuddlan, Flint and Aberystwyth.
3) English law and English officials were appointed in areas formerly belonging to the Welsh rulers.
4) The rulers of Powys and Deheubarth were now servants of the King of England.

Dafydd was given lands east of the Conway River as a reward for helping the English. However, during the next few years, the Welsh began to complain at the way in which they were being mistreated by English officials. As a result, Dafydd decided to rebel. He and his men attacked and burned the town of Hawarden on Palm Sunday 1282. The rebellion spread to every district in Wales which was under Edward I's control.

Llywelyn decided to join the rebellion. As a result, Edward declared war and invaded Wales with a massive army. He again invaded Gwynedd from three different directions. This time, the English failed to capture Anglesey. This victory encouraged Llywelyn to counter attack the English. He led his men out of their mountain stronghold towards Builth in central Wales. It was near Builth, at an isolated spot called Cilmeri that Llywelyn was killed on 11 December 1282.

E A map of Wales showing Edward I's invasion routes, 1267-77

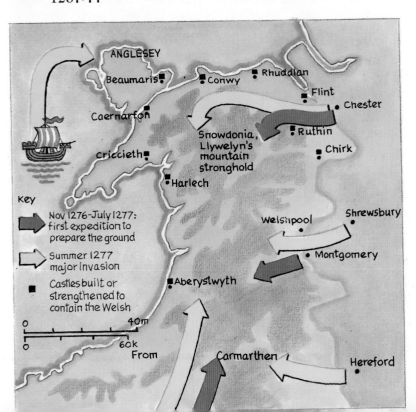

Two poems written about the death of Llywelyn

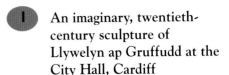

I An imaginary, twentieth-century sculpture of Llywelyn ap Gruffudd at the City Hall, Cardiff

With Llywelyn's death, gone is my mind
Heart frozen in the breast with terror,
Desire decays like dried-up branches,
See you not the rush of wind and rain?
See you not the oaks lash each other?
See you not the ocean scourging the shore?
See you not the truth is portending?
See you not that the stars have fallen?

Here lies the prince of errors.
A traitor and a thief,
A flaring, flaming firebrand,
The malefactor's chief.
The Wild evil genius.
Who sought the good to kill,
Dregs of the faithless Trojans.
And source of every ill.

F *(above)* A poem by William Rishanger, a monk of St Albans

G *(left)* Gruffudd ap yr Ynad Coch, a Welsh poet, wrote this poem on hearing of Llywelyn's death

Was Llywelyn bound to lose?

If their princes could come to an agreement and unite and defend their country - or better still, if they had only one prince a good one - living as they do in a country so inaccessible and so well protected, I cannot see how powerful a people could ever be completely conquered. If they were united, no one could ever beat them. They have three great advantages: their country is fortified by nature; they are used to living on very little and the whole nation is trained in the use of arms. The English forces are hired soldiers, the Welsh are defending their homeland.

H Gerald of Wales's view

Yet in truth, the chances of the survival of Wales, even a smaller Wales, as an independent unit were virtually nil … Once the English monarchy fully concentrated its power on Wales, the days of its independence were numbered.

J R R Davies, a modern Welsh historian, disagreed with Gerald of Wales's view (source H)

1 Discuss, in groups, the following:
When Dafydd ap Gruffudd rebelled against Edward I in 1282, what should Llywelyn have done? Should he have:
(a) Stayed out of the conflict (remember that Edward had crushed Llywelyn in 1277);
(b) Joined up with Edward against Dafydd (remember that Dafydd had betrayed Llywelyn even though he was his brother);
(c) Joined up with Dafydd against Edward I (remember that Dafydd was leading a nation-wide rebellion and that Llywelyn was still Prince of Wales)?
Why do you think that Llywelyn chose the third option?

2 Read the two poem extracts in sources F and G. They are expressing the feelings of the writers. Of what value are they as historical sources?

3 How do you know that source C is in favour of Llywelyn whilst source D is against him?

4 Look at source I. This is an imaginary sculpture of Llywelyn ap Gruffudd by a modern day artist. How is Llywelyn portrayed? Why do you think he is portrayed in this way?

5 'Llywelyn was bound to lose.' Divide into two groups, one in favour of this statement, the other against it. List your main reasons and give examples to support each one.

39

II How far had Wales and Britain changed by 1300?

A A map of Wales in 1284

Justiciars of South Wales
1298 – Walter Pederton
1300 – John Havering
1301 – Walter Hakelut
1305 – Walter Pederton
Beadles of Mabelfyw
1287-88 – Llywelyn ap Gruffudd
1301-1302 – Dafydd ap Madog

A closer look at Wales: the Principality

By 1300 every trace of Welsh independence had been rubbed out. Edward I had taken Llywelyn ap Gruffudd's crown and kept it at Westminster Abbey. Llywelyn's only child had been sent away to become a nun. His only surviving brother, Rhodri, had been forced to live in England. In 1301, Edward declared his own son, also called Edward, to be 'Prince of Wales'.

English towns

Edward set up towns around the castles that he built. Only English people could live there. The Welsh people, who were already living in these areas, had to move out. If the the Welsh wanted to buy and sell their goods, they could only do so in these towns. They were known as royal boroughs.

English law

According to the **Statute** of Rhuddlan, proclaimed by Edward I in 1284, English law was imposed on Wales. English judges were appointed and English courts were created. But Welsh law was allowed to continue in some instances. For example, when a nobleman died his land would still be shared amongst his sons.

English officials

English officials were put in charge of the **Principality** of Wales. The **Justiciar** of North Wales resided at Caernarfon Castle and the Justiciar of South Wales at Carmarthen Castle. Gwynedd and Deheubarth were divided into shires; Anglesey, Caernarfonshire, Merionethshire and Flintshire, Cardiganshire and Carmarthenshire. Each county was run by a **sheriff** who took his orders from the Justiciar. The sheriff collected fines and taxes but there were other officials, such as the beadle and the reeve, beneath the sheriff and they were often Welshmen.

---

1 Compare source B with source C on page 5. Describe any one change which had taken place in Wales, England, Scotland and Ireland, paying attention to the way in which they were organised and ruled.

2 Make a list of the changes that took place in Wales as a result of English conquest.

3 (a) What information is there in these pages that shows the system set up by Edward I was unpopular?
  (b) What information is there in these pages that shows the system set up by Edward was acceptable to the Welsh?

4 Why do you think towns were built around Edward I's castles?

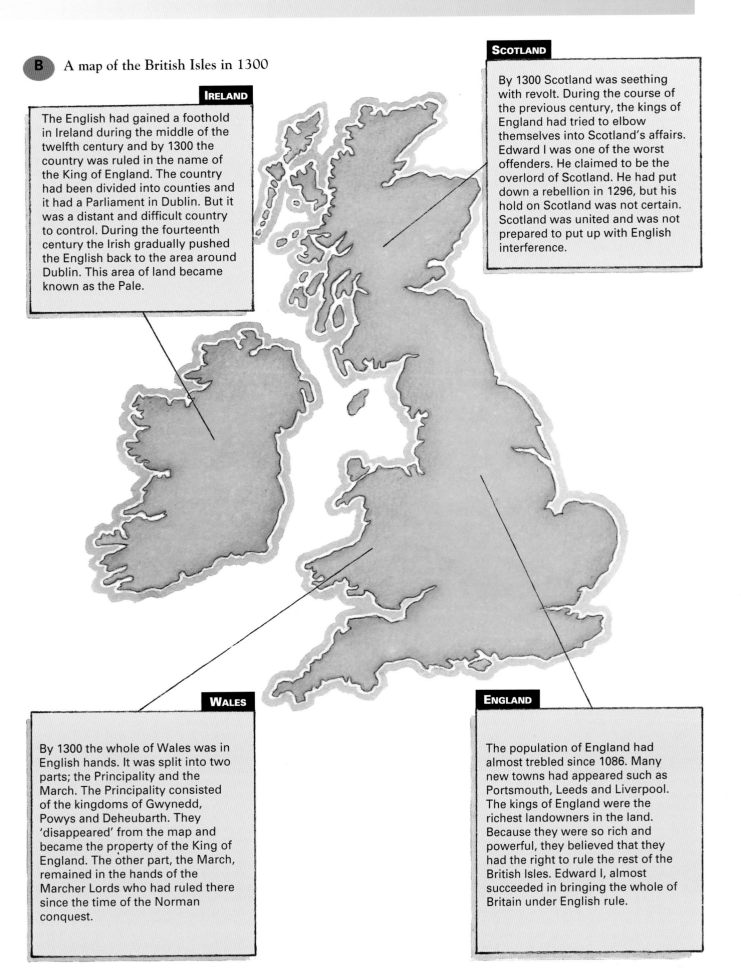

B A map of the British Isles in 1300

IRELAND

The English had gained a foothold in Ireland during the middle of the twelfth century and by 1300 the country was ruled in the name of the King of England. The country had been divided into counties and it had a Parliament in Dublin. But it was a distant and difficult country to control. During the fourteenth century the Irish gradually pushed the English back to the area around Dublin. This area of land became known as the Pale.

SCOTLAND

By 1300 Scotland was seething with revolt. During the course of the previous century, the kings of England had tried to elbow themselves into Scotland's affairs. Edward I was one of the worst offenders. He claimed to be the overlord of Scotland. He had put down a rebellion in 1296, but his hold on Scotland was not certain. Scotland was united and was not prepared to put up with English interference.

WALES

By 1300 the whole of Wales was in English hands. It was split into two parts; the Principality and the March. The Principality consisted of the kingdoms of Gwynedd, Powys and Deheubarth. They 'disappeared' from the map and became the property of the King of England. The other part, the March, remained in the hands of the Marcher Lords who had ruled there since the time of the Norman conquest.

ENGLAND

The population of England had almost trebled since 1086. Many new towns had appeared such as Portsmouth, Leeds and Liverpool. The kings of England were the richest landowners in the land. Because they were so rich and powerful, they believed that they had the right to rule the rest of the British Isles. Edward I, almost succeeded in bringing the whole of Britain under English rule.

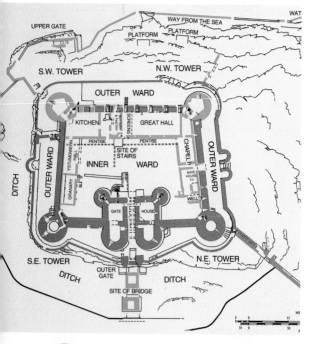

The plan labels include:
UPPER GATE, WAY FROM THE SEA, WAT, PLATFORM, PLATFORM, S.W. TOWER, N.W. TOWER, OUTER WARD, KITCHEN, GREAT HALL, SCREENS, PENTISE, PENTISE, CHAPEL, OUTER WARD, DITCH, OUTER WARD, YSTRADGWYN HALL, SITE OF STAIRS, INNER WARD, GRANARY, WELL, BAKE HOUSE, GATE HOUSE, S.E. TOWER, DITCH, OUTER GATE, DITCH, N.E. TOWER, SITE OF BRIDGE

A A plan of Harlech Castle

B A modern day photograph of Harlech Castle

Royal English castles

By 1300 Edward I had surrounded the old kingdom of Gwynedd with a chain of huge stone castles. These castles were situated in Aberystwyth, Builth, Beaumaris, Caernarfon, Conway, Flint, Harlech, Rhuddlan and Ruthin. Their purpose was to keep a close eye on the Welsh, making sure that if they rose in rebellion, they could easily be defeated.

Edward spent a fortune on these castles – £80,000, a sum equivalent to £10 million in today's money. His chief architect was Master James of St George, a gifted castle builder from the French border town of Savoy. His designs were based on the concentric principle. Concentric castles had extremely strong towers and gatehouses along with two rings of thick, defensive walls. If the enemy managed to get through the outer wall, they could easily be picked off by soldiers defending the inner wall.

Harlech Castle is a good example of a concentric ring castle. Harlech was built over a seven year period between 1283 and 1290. Almost 1000 workers were employed on the building. The workforce consisted of masons, diggers and carpenters. They were brought to the site from all parts of England and were forced to work there. Master James chose the site carefully – a high, rocky crag jutting out from the sea.

The strength of Harlech Castle was put to the test in 1295, when the Welsh rose in rebellion under Madog ap Llywelyn. The revolt lasted for nine months. Madog besieged Harlech but, try as they might, the Welsh failed to capture it because the English defenders could be supplied with food by sea.

C *(left)* Building workers receiving their pay

D *(below)* The impressment of workmen for the king's castles in North Wales 1282-83

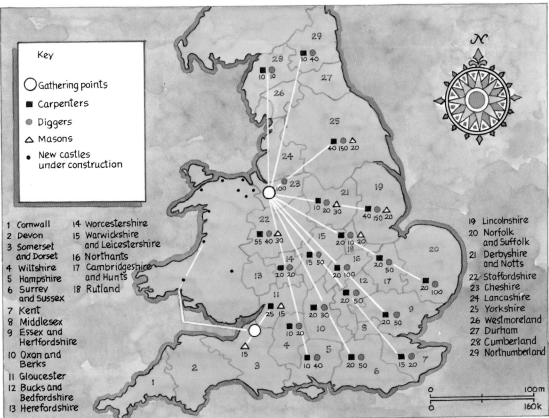

Key

○ Gathering points
■ Carpenters
● Diggers
△ Masons
• New castles under construction

1 Cornwall
2 Devon
3 Somerset and Dorset
4 Wiltshire
5 Hampshire
6 Surrey and Sussex
7 Kent
8 Middlesex
9 Essex and Hertfordshire
10 Oxon and Berks
11 Gloucester
12 Bucks and Bedfordshire
13 Herefordshire
14 Worcestershire
15 Warwickshire and Leicestershire
16 Northants
17 Cambridgeshire and Hunts
18 Rutland
19 Lincolnshire
20 Norfolk and Suffolk
21 Derbyshire and Notts
22 Staffordshire
23 Cheshire
24 Lancashire
25 Yorkshire
26 Westmoreland
27 Durham
28 Cumberland
29 Northumberland

1 (a) **Name the castles built by Edward I in Wales. Why were they built?**
  (b) **Give three reasons why they were situated near the sea.**
  (c) **Describe the strengths of Harlech Castle.**

2 (a) **Why were only English workmen used for building the castles in Wales?**
  (b) **Why did they have to be forced to work in Wales?**

3 (a) **Look at source D. Which counties supplied the greatest number of workmen?**
  (b) **Why was Chester a convenient gathering point?**

4 **Describe what is happening in source C.**

5 **You are a Welsh nobleman living in 1300. Describe fully the changes that have taken place since 1282. (Refer to pages 40 and 41 as well.)**

Gerald of Wales's descriptions of the Welsh way of life:

> *Most of the farming is pastoral; they grow very little crops.*

 A Agriculture

> *... the whole population lives almost entirely on oats and the produce of their herds, milk, cheese and butter. They eat plenty of meat, but little bread. They pay no attention to commerce, shipping or industry ...*

B The people's diet

> *In Wales no one begs. Everyone's home is open to all ... Guests who arrive early are entertained until nightfall by girls who play to them on the harp.*

C Entertainment

D An artist's impression of the land belonging to a typical Marcher Lord

A closer look at Wales: the March

Large parts of Wales had been conquered by English barons long before 1282. As we have seen, their lands were known as the **March**. They were run differently from lands in England.

The Marcher territories consisted of two main areas – the low lying area, where the land was at its richest, and the poorer, more mountainous area with its woodland and moors. The lowland territory was known as the Englishry, inhabited mainly by English and Norman settlers, and the higher land was known as the Welshry, where the Welsh people lived.

The Marcher Lords of Wales were more powerful than the barons in England. They were supposed to serve the King of England, but in practice, they were able to behave like lesser kings in their own right, leading their own armies whenever they wanted and operating their own laws and customs.

Each of the Marcher Lords kept the best land to himself and shared out the rest amongst his knights. They paid the lord by serving in his army. The knights organised their 'fees' (pieces of land) into manors. The manor consisted of the lord's manor house, the church and the village where the peasants lived. Surrounding the manor were a number of large, open-ended fields – these comprised the lord's land called the **demesne**, three open fields where crops were grown, meadow land where the farm animals grazed, and wasteland.

On the manor each field was divided into strips and every peasant was given a number for their own use, which were scattered about the three fields. Every year one of the fields was allowed to lie fallow, which meant that nothing could be grown on it. This was to

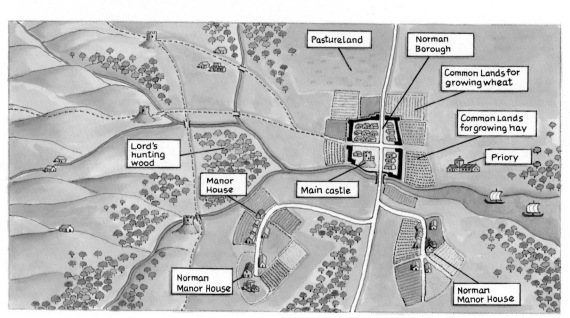

Pastureland

Norman Borough

Common Lands for growing wheat

Common Lands for growing hay

Priory

Lord's hunting wood

Manor House

Main castle

Norman Manor House

Norman Manor House

ensure that the soil did not lose any of its goodness. Animals provided natural fertilisers because they were allowed to graze on the weeds which grew in the field.

This system appears to have been fair, but in practice, it was the opposite. The **serfs** got the worst deal. They were not free to come and go as they wanted to. They were tied to the land and to the lords (as they were the owners of the land). As well as the inconvenience of having to work on the lord's land, they had to pay him for using his mill. They could not hunt on his game reserve and to cap it all they had to pay a tenth of their income to the Church.

The holy days of the Church were important dates in the calendar. People were allowed days off during these festivals. Later on, the words 'holy' and 'day' became holiday, and it was a time when the villagers danced and played sports.

In the Welshry, provided they did not cause trouble, the Welsh were allowed to keep to their own laws and traditional way of life. But life, for most of the people, remained just as bad as it had always been. The soil was poor and the Welsh had to depend upon keeping livestock for their livelihood.

They saw an old black high hall … with lots of smoke coming from it. And when they entered the hall, they saw an uneven raised floor that was full of holes, which a man could walk on only with the greatest difficulty because it was so full of cow's dung and urine … And the hallway of the house was damp and grey … And on the other side of the fire there was a yellow calf's skin … it was a great honour to be able to sit on this.

E This description, thought to have been written during the thirteenth century, comes from an old Welsh legend, the *Dream of Rhonabwy*

F A Welsh house in the Middle Ages

1 Write in your words what we mean by the word manor.

2 Why do you think the Marcher Lords left the Welsh people in the upland areas free to get on with their own lives?

3 (a) Describe the ways in which life on the manor in the Englishry was different from life in the Welshry.
   (b) State the ways in which they were similar.

4 Study the sources relating to the Welsh way of life and write your own description of it.

5 In what ways do you think life for people living in the Principality was different from life in the Welsh Marches? In what ways was it similar?

12 Cosmeston: reconstructing a medieval village

Historians study sources. Sometimes these sources are written, but they do not always have to be in words. Sources can be in the form of physical objects, or materials, that have survived from the past. Historians who study the physical remains are called **archaeologists**.

In 1977 some archaeologists discovered, after digging into the ground, lines of stones near Sully in the Vale of Glamorgan. They believed that these stones were the remains of stone houses which were part of a village dating back to the fourteenth century.

How did they know this?

Firstly, they found bits of pottery in the same area as the stones. The pottery dated back to the late Middle Ages. Secondly, they found a silver penny portraying Edward I. The penny belonged to the year 1297. Thirdly, within a stone's throw of the village, the remains of a manor house have been found, as well as a dovecot and a bee garden. (These remains are best seen from the air, as shown in source A). A document stated that the manorhouse was a ruin by the year 1437.

The archaeologists studied a written document which described the lives of the Lords of Sully from the year 1166. This document referred to a village called Constentinstune, named after a man called de Constentin. He was a Norman soldier who fought at the Battle of Hastings in 1066. He accompanied Robert Fitzhamon, the Norman lord who conquered Glamorgan, during the latter part of

A An aerial photograph of the Cosmeston site shows the distinctive features of the village

B (below) The archaeologists' conclusions about the Cosmeston site, based on evidence they found

1) The village must have been built after the Norman conquest. There is no trace of a village having existed before that time.
2) The village must have been inhabited for several generations, stretching from the eleventh century until the middle of the fourteenth cenury – a total of about 350 years.
3) The village of Cosmeston was one of a small group of villages belonging to the manor of the de Constetin family.
4) The villagers must have been serfs working on land belonging to de Constentin, who lived in the manor house nearby.
5) The serfs were likely to have come from England. The village formed part of the Englishry of the Lordship of Glamorgan.
6) The population of the village must have gone into decline through famine.
7) Historians know that the climate at the beginning of the fourteenth century began to change. The winters became colder and longer, the summers wetter and shorter. This hit harvests badly. In a village like Cosmeston, it meant that there was less food for the farm animals
8) In turn the lack of animal feed meant that there was less manure to fertilise the soil. It became a vicious circle. There was less and less food to go round.
9) To cap it all, in the middle of the fourteenth century the Black Death struck. It must either have killed off the villagers or forced them to move to other villages where the soil was richer.

C An artist's impression of a house as it would have appeared in medieval Cosmeston

D A photograph of one of the reconstructed houses at Cosmeston

the eleventh century. As part of the feudal system, Costentin was given a piece of land by Fitzhamon. Using this evidence, the archaeologists came to the conclusions shown in source B.

Cosmeston has been re-created and in order to convey to visitors what life was like in medieval times, guides can be seen dressed up as medieval people. In source E the guide is dressed up as the village reeve. The reeve was a kind of village boss who spoke with the lord of the manor on the villagers' behalf.

The insides of the villager's houses were very plain. None of the houses had a proper chimney, a hole was placed in the roof and a fire was made on the bare floor below it. Women had very specific roles in the home and their main responsibilities were to cook food and to raise the children. All of the villagers' livelihoods depended on keeping farm animals and on growing wheat in the fields which surrounded the village.

E The village reeve

1 This is how Gerald of Wales described the houses of the Welsh people, '... they do not build ... lofty stone buildings, but content themselves with small huts made of the boughs of trees twisted together ...'
In what way does this contradict the evidence found by the archaeologists at Cosmeston?

2 Do the differences between Gerald's description (see question 1) and the evidence uncovered at Cosmeston mean that we cannot accept Gerald's evidence? (Clues: local limestone and clay.)

3 The village was built in an area where the soil was not as good as in other parts of the Vale of Glamorgan. What conclusion can you draw from this? (Clue: population.)

4 (a) Do you think that physical evidence is more reliable than written evidence?
(b) Why do you think that the people living in Cosmeston left no written evidence?

5 The archaeologists decided to re-create the village of Cosmeston on the basis of the sources which they had discovered. How do you think they went about this task?

6 (a) The village did not contain any shops. Why do you think this was so?
(b) Why do you think the village was so small?

7 Do these sources show how hard life was for the villagers of Cosmeston in the Middle Ages?

*13 T*he fourteenth century: a time of turmoil

A A statue of Robert Bruce at Bannockburn. He died of leprosy in 1329

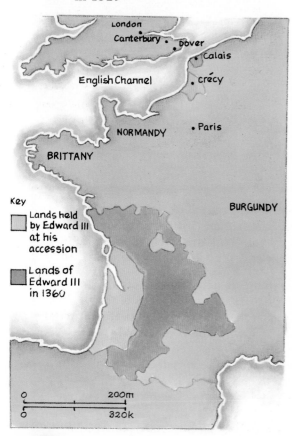

Key

Lands held by Edward III at his accession

Lands of Edward III in 1360

London
Canterbury
Dover
Calais
English Channel
Crécy
NORMANDY
Paris
BRITTANY
BURGUNDY

0 — 200m
0 — 320k

B A map of France during the 100 Years War, showing Edward III's territorial gains by 1360

War between England and Scotland

Scotland, unlike Wales, was a united country, under the rule of one king. It was further away from London than Wales, and was a bigger and richer country, containing many towns. Scotland therefore was a much more difficult country to conquer. But this did not stop Edward I.

After conquering Wales in 1282, Edward turned his attention to the affairs of Scotland. The Scots disliked the interference of the English king and they rose in revolt under their leader William Wallace. Wallace defeated the English at the Battle of Stirling Bridge in 1297. However, two years later Edward got his own back and defeated the Scots at the Battle of Falkirk. He used Welsh archers in this battle. Wallace was captured and finally executed in 1305. Edward I became known as 'the Hammer of the Scots'.

Edward became the ruler of Scotland and took the Stone of Scone to London. This stone was used in the crowning ceremony of the Scottish king and was a symbol of the independence of Scotland. Before long, the Scots were in revolt again. This time their leader was Robert Bruce. The Scots chose him as their king. Edward II, who became King of England in 1307, was not as strong as his father and Robert Bruce succeeded in seizing almost every castle in Scotland.

In 1314, with 20,000 men behind him, Robert Bruce met Edward II and the English army at the Battle of Bannockburn. Here, the English were decisively defeated and Scotland regained its independence.

War between England and France

During Edward III's reign, England declared war against the King of France. Edward claimed the country's crown. He was also anxious to defend his lands in the south west of France because English merchants did a lot of trading with these areas. Edward was supported by the barons and the merchants of England. This war was called the Hundred Years War, this was because the fighting lasted, off and on, from 1337 until 1453.

Wales and the Hundred Years War

Welsh longbowmen were especially valuable during these wars. They played a big role in the first large land battle of the war, the Battle of Crécy, fought in 1346. These longbowmen were so deadly that a skilled archer could fire 12 arrows per minute and the mounted knights had to wear plate armour to defend themselves.

C This picture shows the siege of Mortagne. Owain *Lawgoch* is seen dying from an arrow wound. The illustration appears in the *Chronicle d'Angleterre* by Jean de Wavrin, which dates from the fifteenth century

The Battle of Crécy was a victory for Edward III. In 1356, at the Battle of Poitiers, the French were again defeated. The English forces were led by the king's son, Edward the Prince of Wales, commonly known as the Black Prince.

Owain *Lawgoch* – Owain the Red Hand

Another famous Welshman who fought in the war was Owain *Lawgoch* or Owain the Red Hand. Owain was the grandson of Rhodri, the brother of Llywelyn ap Gruffudd, and he claimed to be the rightful Prince of Wales. His claim was supported by the French. Owain formed his own company of soldiers and fought under the banner of the King of France. In 1372, the King of France decided to help Owain invade Wales. The invasion never came about. Owain got as far as the island of Guernsey, but he had to turn back in order to fight against the English in France. Six years later, in 1378, Owain was assassinated by a traitor, named John Lamb, whilst fighting the English.

During the fifteenth century, Welshmen like Dafydd Gam and Matthew Goch fought bravely on the English side. By 1453, however, the English had lost the wars and had to pull out of France.

During the siege of Mortagne, Owain used to sit in front of the castle … One fine morning he sat on the trunk of a tree and told John Lamb to fetch his comb … As he returned with the comb, the devil must have entered his body, for with his comb he bought a dagger and he struck it into Owain, whose body was almost naked and killed him.

D An account, by Froissart, of the death of Owain *Lawgoch*

1 What part did the following people play in Scotland's struggle against Edward I:
   (a) William Wallace;
   (b) Robert Bruce?

2 Draw a timeline, noting on it the main events in the struggle between the Scots and the English.

3 Why do you think the French were friendly with the Scots and were also willing to support Owain *Lawgoch* in his bid to free Wales?

4 Look at the map shown in source B. In what way did England's position change in France between 1336 and 1453?

5 Study source C. Describe in detail what is happening in this scene.

At the beginning, both men and women were affected by a sort of swelling in the groin or under the armpits, which sometimes reached the size of a common apple or egg. Some of these swellings were larger than this and some were smaller. They were commonly called boils. From these two starting points, the boils began in a little while to spread all over the body. Later, the appearance of the disease changed to black or red patches on the arms and thighs. These blotches quickly led to death.

A   **A description of the plague, written by Boccaccio**

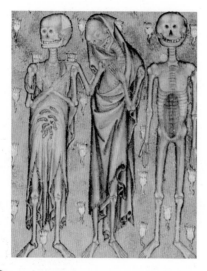

B   **A contemporary image of the Great Death**

C   **The effects of the plague on social relations**

The Great Death

The Great Death is the name given to a dreadful disease which appeared in the middle of the fourteenth century. Later on it was called the Black Death. Source A was written by the Italian writer Boccaccio and gives us a graphic picture of what the illness was like.

The disease first appeared in China in 1313, and from there it spread to Europe. In 1349, it first appeared on the south coast of England. It spread like wildfire through the rest of the country and spread to Wales from the port of Bristol. The disease also reached Scotland and Ireland.

People at that time thought that the plague was God's way of punishing people for their wrongdoings. There were doctors at that time, but they were few and far between and their knowledge was very primitive. They had no remedies for the illness, no idea of the existence of bacteria and they certainly did not know that these bacteria were carried by flea-infested, black rats. The rats were found on board ships, travelling from Asia to the ports of Europe. Anybody catching the disease would be dead within a matter of days. The slightest cough by a sufferer would spread the germs to other people in their vicinity.

The effects of the plague

The main result of the plague was that it led to a large drop in the population. In England, it is reckoned that it killed off one third of the population – one person in every three. The same thing happened in Wales and in every other country in Europe.

Many of the people who died were serfs and agricultural labourers. This meant that there were far fewer workers to do the work in the fields, and in turn this meant that there was far less food being produced. The situation created problems for the king, bishops and barons who owned the land. Sources D, F and G list the effects of the Great Death in Wales alone.

The owners did one of two things (see source C):

1) Some owners forced the few serfs who survived the plague to work harder on the lords' own lands.
2) Some owners gave the serfs who survived their freedom.

This meant that instead of having to work on the lord's land for nothing, they were paid for doing it.

In some areas, the serfs were free even before the coming of the plague. Many of these serfs, provided they survived the plague, began to demand a rise in their wages. Many lords gave in to them. In this way, the decline of the manor system was speeded up by the Black Death.

Another effect of the plague was that it made some people even more religious than they were already. They whipped themselves, thinking that by inflicting punishment upon themselves God would look kindly on them. They went on pilgrimages to holy places. On the other hand, there were some people who became pessimistic about everything, thinking that there was no point in going on living. They became pleasure seeking (see source E.)

	1348			1352		
	£	s	d	£	s	d
Abergavenny Borough	135	3	0	106	3	4
Englishton	65	0	6	61	7	6
Llangattock	30	12	8	22	6	9
The forestry of the mountains	41	3	0	3	0	0

F Total value of taxes in the lands of the lordship of Abergavenny before and after the plague of 1349

And for three reaping works at Brentes which used to reap the lord's corn for three days without food; nothing because the said tenants are dead and their tenements lie waste between the lord's lands for lack of tenants.

G The effects of plague were felt by the landowners

The plague took the lives
of my gentle darlings …
Handsome Ieuan was taken
nine years before the others;
and now the worst turn of all has happened,
… Morfudd was taken, fair Dafydd was taken,
Ieuan, everyone's cheery favourite, was taken,
with an unceasing lament Dyddgu was taken,
and I was left, feeling betrayed and stunned …

D This extract comes from in a poem written by a fourteenth-century poet, Llywelyn Fychan. The poem is called *The Pestilence* and it describes the poet's feelings about the death of his children during the plague

Others believed that plenty of drinking and enjoyment, singing and free-living was the best way to prevent the plague. Day and night they went from one tavern to another, drinking and carousing.

E Boccaccio, describing life in the city of Florence in Italy in 1350

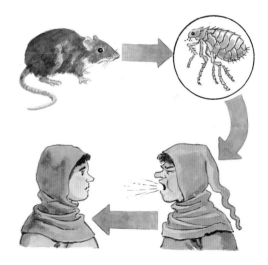

H How the Great Death was spread

1 **Read source A. Why was the Great Death later to become known as the Black Death?**

2 **Look at source B. In what way does it create a sense of fear in the eyes of the beholder?**

3 **In what ways do you think the Great Death created bad feelings between the lords and and the ordinary people?**

4 (a) **'The Great Death was a disaster'. Write an argument in favour of this statement.**

(b) **Write an argument against the same statement. Make sure that you use all the information to be found in this chapter in both your answers.**

Labourers who are idle and not willing to work after the plague without very high wages shall be ordered to work, receiving the usual wages. Labourers refusing to work in this way should be punished by imprisonment.

A An extract from the Statute of Labourers

I saw a poor man near me hanging onto his plough:
His coat was of a cloth that was 'cary',
His hood was full of holes and his hair stuck out,
Through his worn shoes with their thick soles,
His toes peeped out as he trod the land:
His stockings hung down his shins on every side,
All dirtied with mud as he followed the plough.
Two mittens he wore, made all of patches,
The fingers were worn through and covered with mud.

B A poem by Piers Plowman describing a serf

C A map of England during the Peasants' Revolt

The Peasants' Revolt

Why did the peasants revolt?

The wars between England and France were very costly. King Edward III had to spend large sums of money paying the army's wages. He raised this money by forcing the people to pay taxes. These were very unpopular. Life after the Great Death was hard enough as it was, but taxes made matters much worse and the king had the backing of Parliament. However, Parliament did not speak for the mass of the ordinary people. Only bishops, lords, knights and townspeople could belong to it. The wishes of the ordinary people were ignored.

In 1351, Parliament, with the support of the king, passed the Statute of Labourers. This law was intended to help the lords control their peasants. It stated that labourers could not expect any increase in their wages. (See source A.)

Then, in 1377, King Richard II, Edward II's grandson, imposed an extra tax with the backing of Parliament. It was called the Poll Tax. Everybody, rich and poor alike, had to pay 12d (5p) each. Anybody refusing to pay it could be thrown into prison. As far as the peasants were concerned, this was the last straw.

Tax gatherers went from one village to another collecting the Poll Tax from every person. Some people managed to hide, but others were caught. One of the unlucky people was a priest called John Ball. He preached that the tax was unfair because everybody had to pay the same amount, rich and poor alike. He argued that this went against Christ's teaching in the Bible. The Church, however, supported the tax. Ball was arrested and was thrown into Canterbury jail.

What happened in 1381?

In 1381, thousands of peasants from Essex and Kent rose in revolt. The Kent rebels released John Ball and chose as their leader an old soldier named Wat Tyler. The rebels marched to London and reached the outskirts of the city on the southern banks of the River Thames. The Essex rebels were camped on the northern side of the city.

Richard II was only 14 years of age and he did not have enough soldiers to defend the City of London. He also knew that there were plenty of poor people living in London itself who would be only too glad to support the rebels. Richard hid in the Tower of London and whilst there he decided to meet the rebels. He sailed in a boat up the River Thames but when he saw the rebels, he panicked and sailed back to the Tower without having met Wat Tyler.

The rebels entered the City and broke into the Archbishop of Canterbury's palace. They then attacked lawyers and foreign merchants and started general looting. It was only a matter of time before they reached the Tower of London. In the face of this crisis, Richard decided to meet with the Kent rebels at Mile End, just outside the City. Richard gave in to all the rebels' demands. He promised to do away with the Poll tax and agreed to allow the peasants more freedom. Whilst this meeting was being held, another group of rebels broke into the Tower and murdered the Archbishop of Canterbury. The king then decided to meet the rebels again, and to have a face to face talk with Wat Tyler at Smithfield.

At the beginning of this meeting, there was a scuffle involving Tyler, during the course of which he was murdered. Most of the accounts written at that time sided with the king. Sources D and E give conflicting views of the same events.

The king then bravely confronted the rebels and succeeded in calming them by promising once more to make life better for them. In the face of the king's plea, the rebels decided to return to their homes. However, once life had returned to normal, the king broke his promises. The leaders of the revolt were executed, including John Ball. Nonetheless the Poll Tax was eventually abolished.

The aims of the rebels were not fulfilled immediately after they had revolted, but within a hundred years, most of the labourers had been given their freedom.

At Smithfield John Newton, a knight, came up to Wat [whom he] approached … on horseback and not on foot. Newton said, 'As you are sitting on a horse it is not insulting for me to approach you on a horse.' At this Wat threatened to stab the knight and called him a traitor. The knight called Wat a liar and drew a knife too. The King ordered Newton to get down from his horse and hand over his knife. But Tyler still tried to attack the knight so the Mayor of London and many royal knights and squires came to the aid of the King. Then the King took courage and ordered the Mayor to arrest Tyler. The Mayor arrested Tyler and struck him a blow on the head. Tyler was soon surrounded by the other servants of the King and was pierced by sword thrusts in several parts of the body.

D This version was written by a monk living at St Albans, named Thomas Walshingham. He was not present at this meeting but was told about it by someone else

E *(left)* King Richard II meeting Wat Tyler and the rebels at Smithfield. This picture appears in Froissart's *Chronicles* and was drawn one hundred years after the event. The picture depicts the king twice, once dealing with Tyler and the second time addressing the crowd

---

1 Describe the roles played by Wat Tyler and John Ball in the Peasants' Revolt.

2 What were the aims of the rebels?

3 What evidence is there that the rebellion was not planned?

4 (a) What impression is the artist in source E trying to create?
   (b) What do you notice about the peasants in the picture? Why do you think have they been painted like this?

5 (a) Read source D and study source E. In what ways do they agree with each other?
   (b) In what ways do they disagree with each other?

6 (a) In the face of the rebels entering London, did Richard II have any choice but to give in to them? Give reasons for your answer.
   (b) Why do you think the rebels were prepared to kill the Archbishop of Canterbury but were not willing to kill the king?

14 Poets and poetry in the Middle Ages

And the Lord Rhys held a great festival at the castle of Cardigan, wherein he appointed two sorts of competition between the poets, and the other between the harpers, fiddlers, pipers, and various performers of instrumental music, and he gave two chairs for the winners in the competitions, and these he enriched with vast gifts.

 A An extract from *Chronicle of the Princes* describing an *eisteddfod* held at Cardigan in 1176

Their poems are so inventive and ingenious, that, when using their own language, they produce works of art which are attractive and highly original, both in the choice of words and the ideas contained in them.

 B Gerald of Wales emphasised interest in the *eisteddfod* in his book on the Welsh people

How important were poets in medieval Wales?

One of the most important forms of entertainment in Wales was listening to poetry being read aloud by the court poets. Poets had always played a big part in the life of Wales. Before 1282, the best poets lived in the courts of the Welsh kings. Their main role was to write poems praising the king for his bravery and generosity. They enjoyed competing against each other in a special event called an *eisteddfod*.

The Welsh language was spoken in every part of Wales. Most people spoke only Welsh. Edward I did not try to stop people speaking their language. Many people who settled in Wales learned Welsh and came to appreciate the country's poetry.

When Wales lost its independence in 1282, there was a danger that the poets would be permanently out of work. In fact, they were just as busy after 1282 as they were before. Instead of praising the kings of Wales, they now wrote poems in favour of the *uchelwyr* (noblemen). Many of them travelled from the hall of one uchelwr to the next. They were given a warm welcome as well as free food and lodgings for their services.

Sometimes, the poets wrote about the legendary heroes of Wales and the rivalry between the Welsh and the English. Source C is an illustration from a medieval manuscript showing the age-old battle between the red dragon of Wales and the white dragon of England.

Amongst these poets was the greatest poet that Wales has ever produced. His name was Dafydd ap Gwilym. He wrote wonderful poems describing the beauty of the countryside and the young women of Wales. Dafydd lived at the time of the Great Death but there is no mention of this in his poetry.

English poetry

The fourteenth century was also an important period in the history of the English language. In the 1380s a poet named Geoffrey Chaucer wrote a long poem about people going on a **pilgrimage**. It was called *The Canterbury Tales*. The language used in *The Canterbury Tales* was Middle English.

Another important person in England, at this time, was William Caxton who introduced the first printing press to England in 1476. He used the language he was familiar with in London. Source F is an example of a story of some merchants who were at sea and who landed to get some food.

 C *(left)* **A manuscript illustration depicting the battle between Wales and England (represented by two dragons)**

*Keep *Horsa's offspring from Fflint,*
Rowena's race from Gwynedd.
No posts for Saxons, my lord,
No pardon for a townsman ...
Take Morgannwg and Gwynedd,
Make one land, Conwy to Nedd.
Should England's dukes be angered
Wales will be there in your need.
*Horsa was one of the Anglo-Saxon kings who invaded Britain in the fifth century

D This extract appears in a poem written by Guto'r Glyn and calls upon Earl William Herbert, one of the leading Welshmen of the fifteenth century, to drive the English out of Wales

Whan that Aprill with his shoures sote
The droghte of March hath perced to the roote ...
And smale foweles maken melodye,
That slepen al the nyght with open ye ...
Thanne longen folk to goon on pilgrimages,..
(When April with its sweet showers
has pierced the drought of March to the root
and small birds make melody,
that sleep all night wih open eye ...
then folk long to go on pilgrimages)

E The opening passage of *The Canterbury Tales* by Geoffrey Chaucer

One of them named Sheffelde came inn-to-an hows and axed for mete; and specyally he axyd for eggys. And the good wyfe answerde, that she could speke no frenshe. And the merchaunt was angry, for he coude speke no frenshe, but wolde have hadde egges, and she understode hym not.

F A contemporary story printed by William Caxton

G An illustration of Geoffrey Chaucer reading his poetry at Windsor

Every oak's high summit rings
With the young birds' lusty carollings,
And every copse is sweet with song
And cuckoo calls, the bright day is long,
And a white haze, when the wind dies,
Over the heart of the valley lies,
And evening skies are blue and clear,
And the trees ashimmer with gossamer

H A poem by Dafydd ap Gwilym

---

1 Write about the contribution of the following to the cultural life of Wales and England:
   (i) the *eisteddfod*;
   (ii) Dafydd ap Gwilym;
   (iii) Geoffrey Chaucer;
   (iv) William Caxton.

2 (a) Why were the poets of Wales a dangerous group of people to the King of England?
   (b) In what way is the message in source C similar to that in source D?

3 Why do you think that Dafydd ap Gwilym makes no mention of the Black Death in his poems?

4 Write out the sentences from source F in modern English.

5 How useful do you think poetry is for a historian who is studying the Middle Ages?

The Glyndŵr Rebellion

Who was Owain Glyndŵr?

Owain Glyndŵr was no ordinary person. He was born in 1359, the son of a nobleman who owned lands at Glyndyfrdwy and Sycharth, near modern-day Llangollen, on the banks of the River Dee. He was descended, on both his father's and mother's side from the old Welsh kings of Powys and Deheubarth. As well as being well-educated, he also served his time as a soldier in the armies of Richard II in Scotland.

In 1400, Glyndŵr became involved in a quarrel with Lord Grey of Ruthin, a powerful English baron who lived very near to him. Glyndŵr claimed that Grey had stolen some of his lands. When the matter was brought before Henry IV, the new King of England, Henry sided with Grey. So, on 16 September 1400, Owain Glyndŵr proclaimed himself Prince of Wales, and with his followers, he attacked and burned the town of Ruthin and caused damage to a number of other towns on the Welsh border.

What caused the rebellion to happen?

By the end of 1401, the whole of Wales was supporting the Glyndŵr Rebellion. Source B provides some reasons as to why this happened. For the next three years, Glyndŵr and his army swept all before them. They captured many castles, including Harlech and Aberystwyth (which was won in 1404). In 1402, Glyndŵr defeated the English armies at Mynydd Hyddgen and Bryn Glas in central Wales. He captured Lord Grey and Lord Mortimer, who was one of the most important Lords of the March. When Henry IV invaded Wales he failed to catch Glyndŵr, and on one occasion, his army was driven back by torrential storms.

A A portrait of Owain Glyndŵr in the heat of battle, painted towards the end of the nineteenth century

B The different causes of the Glyndŵr Rebellion

The Black Death caused misery and a sense of hopelessness

Welsh towns were controlled by the English

Welsh churchmen were kept out of the best jobs in the Welsh Church

Welsh noblemen were not allowed to run their estates according to Welsh law.

When the 100 Years War started, the ordinary Welsh people had to pay far heavier taxes to the King of England

However, in order to win the war, Glyndŵr knew that he had to capture all of the English castles in Wales, as well as needing to defeat the English army on the battlefield. So, in 1404, he organised a special parliament - the first of its kind in Wales - at Machynlleth, in order to raise more money for his cause. Glyndŵr persuaded the King of France to help him and he also made agreements with Lord Mortimer and Henry Percy, Earl Northumberland, who were by now bitter enemies of Henry IV. They agreed to divide Wales and England into three parts.

With this support behind him, Glyndŵr made plans for the future. He had his own **Royal Seal**, he made the Church in Wales independent from the Church in England, and the best positions were given to Welsh clergymen. Glyndŵr even thought of setting up **universities** in Wales, one in the north and one in the south.

However, in 1406, the tide began to turn against Glyndŵr. He was forced to retreat before Henry IV's army at Worcester (the French army that had been helping him returned home). In the same year, the English won back Anglesey. By the end of 1408, both of the castles at Harlech and Aberystwyth were back in English hands. Lord Mortimer, Glyndŵr's ally, died in 1408 and many of Glyndŵr's own children were either killed or imprisoned. Glyndŵr himself was never caught, but by 1412, the rebellion was more or less over.

Henry IV had proved to be too strong for Glyndŵr. Henry's army was much larger, and his weaponry was more powerful. His son Henry, the Prince of Wales, was also a talented general.

C A map of Wales and England, showing how Owain Glyndŵr planned to create a separate Welsh state under an agreement with Mortimer and Percy

What were the consequences of the rebellion?

Many parts of Wales had been destroyed during the Glyndŵr Rebellion. Many lives had been lost, both on the Welsh and English sides. Harsh laws, called the Penal Laws, were passed against the Welsh people. They said, for example, that no Welshman could live near any of the English towns in Wales, and the Welsh were prevented from getting together in large crowds.

Yet there was a positive side to the Glyndŵr Rebellion. For the first time in their history, the Welsh had fought as a united people. After the rebellion, the poets began to look forward to the future, eager to find a new figure who would lead the Welsh people.

D Owain Glyndŵr's Royal Seal

---

1 (a) What were the long-term causes of the Glyndŵr Rebellion?
  (b) What were the short-term causes?

2 How important was Glyndŵr in the rebellion?

3 What evidence is there in this chapter to indicate that Owain Glyndŵr intended setting up a separate country from England?

4 In your opinion, was the Glyndŵr Rebellion bound to fail? Give reasons for your answer.

5 Why do you think the Penal Laws were passed? Were they passed:
  (a) to punish the Welsh;
  (b) to make sure that they did not rebel again?
  Give reasons for your answer.

16 The end of the Middle Ages: a change for the better?

A Tretower Castle

The roof's tiled at each gable.
There's a chimney that draws well.
Nine halls in true proportion,
And nine wardrobes in each one.
Elegant shops, comely inside.
And stocked as full as Cheapside,
A church cross, lovely limewhite
Chapels and the windows bright.
Each part full, each house in a court,
Orchard, vineyard and whitefort.
The famed hero's rabbit park,
Ploughs and steeds of a monarch.

B The poet Iolo Goch wrote this poem about Owain Glyndŵr's mansion

The Welsh people ... pay no attention to trade, shopping or industry.

C Gerald of Wales: *Description of Wales*

Many changes took place during the period c1000 – c1500.

Housing

For the first two hundred years of the Middle Ages, the Normans had to live in castles. They were cold, draughty and uncomfortable places in which to reside. However, after the final conquest of Wales in 1282, the Anglo-Norman lords no longer needed to live in them. Gradually, they began to build houses next door to their castles, which we have already encountered (see Chapter 11). One of the most famous examples of this in Wales is the castle and manor house of Tretower in Powys (sources A and D). This change from castle to manor also affected the Welsh lords, the *uchelwyr*, as well. Owain Glyndŵr, for example, lived in a fine mansion at Sycharth in North Wales (described in source B).

Trade

At the beginning of the Middle Ages, there was hardly any trade in Wales (see source C). By the fifteenth century, however, there was plenty of trade taking place in most parts of Wales. Towns then were no bigger than the villages of today, but they were busy places and the ports of Wales were thriving.

Cardiff and Carmarthen in the south, imported all sorts of luxury goods from Bristol, Ireland and the Continent. In the north of Wales, ports such as Caernarfon and Conway traded regularly with Liverpool.

D A photograph of Tretower Court

The King grants to the inhabitants of Kidwelly the right to collect tolls on the following goods:

For each cartload of cloth	2 pence
For each pipe of wine	1 penny
For each cartload of wool	4 pence
For each cartload of iron	2 pence
For each cartload of fish	2 pence
For each cartload of bread	1 penny
For each cartload of salt	1 penny

E This source appears in a document written in the reign of Edward I, providing the people of Kidwelly with help in the building of their town hall. It was written in 1280

F The ports of Medieval Wales

G There was also a big improvement in furniture. These illustrations show the kind of furniture used by the lords towards the end of the Middle Ages

H The clothes of the rich and powerful people changed too. These pictures show what happened

1 (a) **What are main differences between Tretower Castle and Court? (See sources A and D).**
   (b) **In what way was Sycharth (described in source B) similar to Tretower Court?**

2 (a) **In your opinion, why did trade develop in Wales during the Middle Ages?**
   (b) **What sort of people benefited most from this growth in trade?**

3 **In what ways did clothes improve during this period?**

He'll pass on nothing but ploughs,
He does not care for quarrels;
He wants no part of warfare,
He'll press no one for what's his;
He'll not treat us too harshly,
He'll drive no injust demands;
It is his role to suffer;
Without him, no life or world.

A   A poem by Iolo Goch

B   *(below)* **An illustration of a ploughman from the *Luttrell Psalter*, (1340)**

Work

By the fifteenth century, most people still relied on the land for their livelihood. The nature of the work had hardly changed at all. It was still backbreaking. Source B shows how hard it was. This picture comes from the *Luttrell Psalter*, and was painted in about 1340. It depicts ploughmen ploughing a field with a team of oxen. It highlights the fact that work for most people remained hard. Notice how rough their clothing is. The Welsh poet Iolo Goch wrote a poem about the ploughman (see source A).

However, there had been one important change in the world of work. By the fifteenth century, many people were paying for their land not by working for the lord, but by paying rent in cash. The lords were hiring labourers to work on their own land. Also, many people who had no land were now free to move from the areas of their birth to nearby villages where they could work for better wages. It was a time of opportunity and to improve your own situation. This was making it possible for people to enjoy a slightly better standard of living.

Yet in spite of this small improvement, there was still a large gap between the rich and the poor. The lords were getting richer. Some of them were using their lands for the keeping of sheep. They could make very large profits from the sale of wool. Some of them were also building up large estates of land and were selling their produce for vast sums of money.

Law and order

After the conquest of Wales in 1282, the laws of the King of England came into force and criminals were brought before the king's officers. After the Glyndŵr Rebellion, a new set of laws came into force, the Penal Laws, passed against Welsh people especially (see Chapters 6 and 15).

Putting the king's laws into practice, however, was not easy. There was no police force at that time. Anyone seeing a crime being committed had to chase after the criminal. If the offender was not caught, the sheriff organised a *posse comitatus*, which was a force of armed men drawn from the county. In the Marcher lands, the lords could do pretty much what they liked. They had their own courts. Criminals who had committed crimes in the Principality could escape to the March and the sheriff could do little to catch them. In the March itself, criminals could pay the lord a fee for protecting them. As a result, highway robbery, cattle stealing, kidnapping and piracy on the River Severn became common. Outlaws were also active, the most famous of which was Dafydd Siencyn who operated from Merionethshire

C A portrait of William Herbert whose family was to have great influence in the governing of Wales

D A thief fleeing from the Principality to the March

Different views of Medieval Wales

The Wales of the squires rapidly took shape in north and south Wales ... Towns, manors, professions became less English. The Welsh language surged forward in the Vale of Glamorgan. The ports of the south, followed by those of the north, became much busier. The families that were to govern Wales for the next 300 years began to emerge, such as the Salisburys, Bulkeleys, Vaughans, the Gruffydds, the Dynefors and the Herbert family.

A This is a description of Wales at the end of the fifteenth century by the historian Gwyn A Williams

Some features were basic throughout the Middle Ages: Europe consisted of peasant villages ... Everywhere a small group of lords dominated and fed itself from the work of the peasantry.

B Robert Bartlett: *The Making of Europe*

In the three and fifty years which separated the death of Gruffudd ap Llywelyn (1063) from that of Owain Glyn Dŵr (c1415) the social and economic changes that took place during those years were more important than the military and political changes.

C R R Davies: Conquest, Coexistence and Changes 1063-1415

In 1282, the kings of England, did not divert [change] the flow of Welsh life from one course into a new one ... It is true that the Welsh were mistreated by the laws of the English Parliament, and by the cruelty of English officials, but life went on along the same lines as before.

D R T Jenkins: *Yr Apêl at Hanes* (The Appeal of History)

---

1 (a) In what ways had the lives of ordinary people improved by the fifteenth century?
  (b) In what ways had their lives stayed the same?

2 Why do you think historians disagree about the changes which took place during the Middle Ages?

3 Draw a timeline showing the main changes which took place in Wales between 1000 and 1500.

4 Write an essay about the main political, social and economic changes which had taken place in Wales.

Glossary

abbot a person in charge of a monastery
archaeologist a person who studies the physical remains of the past

barbican the part of the castle located near the castle gate and drawbridge
battering ram a wooden beam used to demolish castle walls
battlements the top part of a castle wall
burgess a town dweller who had special rights
baron a very important Norman nobleman

chronicle a list of important events
concentric castle a castle which has several walls, built within one another
conspiracy an agreement between two or more persons to act against somebody else
curtain wall a castle wall

demesne a part of the manor owned by the lord
diocese a church district which is the responsibility of a bishop
dormitory sleeping quarters

earl a nobleman
eisteddfod a Welsh cultural festival, devoted to poetry and music
empire a group of two or more countries, controlled by one ruler
excommunicate to be thrown out of the Church

headquarters the centre of an organisation (e.g. government)

interdict a ban on Church services by the Pope
imports products that are brought into the country
invasion violent entry of an enemy into a country

justiciar a governor

kingdom a country that is ruled by a king

law a rule that is made by a king or by a government

mangonel a siege machine used to demolish castles
manuscript a piece of paper that contains hand-written words
March the name given to the borderland between England and Wales
moat a stretch of water surrounding a castle

overlord a lord who has power over other lords

palisade a fence of wooden stakes belonging to early castles
parliament in the Middle Ages it was a meeting place called by the King to make decisions on important matters
parish a church district in the care of a priest
pilgrimage a journey to a holy place
Principality one part of Wales that was ruled, after 1301, by the King of England's eldest son

refectory a dining hall
Royal Seal a piece of wax which indicated the King's approval on a document

serf an ordinary person in the Middle Ages who was forced to work on the land
sheriff a local official
statute another name for a law

tapestry a fabric decorated with pictures or designs
Tenant in Chief the most important landowners who held land from the King of England

university a place of learning

Index